# The Quantum MAUI Blueprint

## The Ultimate Guide to Quantum Computing and Cross-Platform Development

# LUIS N. MURPHY

# TABLE OF CONTENT

# Introduction to Quantum Computing and Cross-Platform Application Development

In this chapter, we lay the groundwork for understanding how quantum computing is poised to revolutionize computation, while also exploring how modern cross-platform application frameworks—specifically .NET MAUI—can serve as a bridge between advanced quantum concepts and practical, everyday application development.

## Overview of Quantum Computing Concepts

Quantum computing harnesses the principles of quantum mechanics to process information in fundamentally new ways compared to classical computers. Unlike classical bits that exist in one of two states (0 or 1), quantum bits—or qubits—can exist in a superposition of states. This means that a qubit can represent 0, 1, or both simultaneously, enabling the simultaneous exploration of multiple computational paths.

Key quantum phenomena that empower these capabilities include:

- **Superposition:**
  The ability of qubits to exist in multiple states at once. This property allows a quantum computer to evaluate many possible outcomes concurrently,

providing exponential parallelism in certain computations.

- **Entanglement:**
  When qubits become entangled, the state of one qubit is directly related to the state of another, no matter how far apart they are. Entanglement is a critical resource in quantum computing and is exploited in algorithms like quantum teleportation and superdense coding.

- **Interference:**
  Quantum interference allows the probability amplitudes of different computational paths to reinforce or cancel each other. By carefully designing quantum circuits, certain computational paths can be amplified while others are suppressed, leading to the solution of complex problems.

- **Quantum Measurement:**
  Measurement in quantum computing is inherently probabilistic. A quantum measurement collapses the superposition of a qubit to one of the basis states, providing an outcome that is used to extract useful information from the quantum algorithm.

These principles form the core of quantum algorithms. Notably, quantum algorithms such as Shor's algorithm for factoring large numbers, Grover's algorithm for unstructured search, and the quantum Fourier transform have demonstrated that quantum computers can potentially solve specific problems much faster than classical counterparts. While large-scale quantum computers are still under development, current research and near-term quantum devices (often referred to as Noisy Intermediate-Scale Quantum, or NISQ devices) have already inspired significant progress and a renewed focus on quantum algorithm design.

# Motivation for Integrating Quantum Computing with Application Frameworks

As quantum computing matures, the need to interface quantum technologies with traditional software systems becomes increasingly apparent. Modern application frameworks—such as .NET MAUI—provide a robust, flexible, and well-supported environment for building cross-platform applications. Integrating quantum computing concepts into these frameworks offers several key advantages:

1. **Bridging the Gap Between Theory and Practice:**
   While quantum computing theory is rich and mathematically intensive, its practical applications often require accessible and user-friendly interfaces. By integrating quantum computing capabilities into a familiar application framework, developers can experiment with quantum algorithms, simulate quantum circuits, and visualize quantum phenomena without needing to delve into the low-level quantum hardware details.

2. **Enhanced User Experience:**
   Cross-platform application frameworks like .NET MAUI are designed to deliver native performance and a consistent user interface across multiple operating systems (iOS, Android, Windows, macOS). When quantum computing simulations or algorithms are embedded within these applications, users can interact with advanced quantum models through intuitive graphical interfaces. This enhances learning, debugging, and even the development of quantum-inspired solutions for real-world problems.

3. **Rapid Prototyping and Deployment:**
   Modern frameworks come with mature ecosystems, rich libraries, and development tools that facilitate rapid prototyping. Developers can quickly build, test, and deploy quantum-enabled applications. This seamless integration helps accelerate innovation, as researchers and developers can iterate on quantum algorithms while leveraging the extensive capabilities of established software development platforms.

4. **Interdisciplinary Collaboration:**

   By marrying quantum computing with application development, experts from different fields—such as quantum physics, software engineering, and UI/UX design—can collaborate more effectively. Application frameworks can serve as a common language, allowing teams to develop tools that not only perform complex quantum computations but also present the results in a user-friendly format that is accessible to non-experts.

5. **Future-Proofing Software Solutions:**

   As quantum hardware continues to evolve, having a software layer that is adaptable and easily updatable becomes crucial. Integrating quantum functionalities into a cross-platform framework ensures that applications can scale alongside advances in quantum computing technology, making it easier to incorporate real quantum processors once they become commercially viable.

# Roadmap of the Book

This book is designed to take you on a comprehensive journey—from the theoretical underpinnings of quantum computing to the practical skills required to build cross-platform applications that leverage quantum algorithms. The roadmap is as follows:

1. **Foundational Chapters:**

   o *Fundamentals of Quantum Mechanics:* We start by revisiting the essential principles of quantum mechanics, including the mathematical foundations and the physical interpretation of qubits, superposition, and entanglement.

   o *Quantum Circuits and Algorithms:* Subsequent chapters introduce quantum circuits and delve into core quantum algorithms. This section bridges theory with practice, showing how abstract quantum concepts translate into operational algorithms like the quantum Fourier transform, Grover's search, and Shor's factoring algorithm.

## 2. Quantum Information and Error Correction:

○ We explore how quantum information is quantified and manipulated, discuss the challenges posed by quantum noise, and present various quantum error correction techniques that are essential for reliable quantum computation.

## 3. Programming Quantum Computers:

○ This section reviews current quantum programming languages and tools. You'll learn about the quantum development ecosystem, including simulators and cloud-based quantum computing services, setting the stage for integrating these capabilities with conventional software development.

## 4. Integrating with .NET MAUI:

○ The second half of the book is dedicated to .NET MAUI—the modern framework for building cross-platform applications using C#. Here, you'll find comprehensive guidance on creating rich user interfaces, applying architectural patterns like MVVM, and ensuring your applications are optimized for performance across devices.

○ We then demonstrate how to connect quantum computing libraries and simulators to a .NET MAUI application. This includes hands-on projects such as building a quantum circuit simulator app, which allows you to visualize and interact with quantum states and algorithms in real time.

## 5. Advanced Topics and Case Studies:

- Later chapters cover advanced techniques in .NET MAUI development, including custom controls, performance optimization, and the integration of additional services (such as AI or real-time data synchronization) to enhance your quantum-enabled applications.

- Finally, a series of case studies and practical projects consolidate your learning, providing real-world examples and best practices for deploying and scaling quantum computing applications across multiple platforms.

6. **Future Trends:**

- The book concludes by looking forward to emerging research and developments in quantum computing and cross-platform application development. We discuss potential future applications, technological trends, and how the convergence of these fields might reshape industries ranging from finance to healthcare.

This introductory chapter sets the stage for the rest of the book. Whether you are a researcher eager to explore the theoretical limits of quantum computing or a developer looking to integrate cutting-edge quantum algorithms into modern mobile and desktop applications, this book is designed to provide you with both the conceptual background and the practical skills necessary for the quantum computing revolution.

# Fundamentals of Quantum Mechanics

Quantum mechanics is the theoretical framework that underpins our modern understanding of nature at the smallest scales. It challenges classical intuitions with phenomena that seem almost magical—particles that can be in multiple places at once, correlations that defy local realism, and a probabilistic nature of physical processes. In this section, we explore the essential concepts of quantum mechanics, focusing on quantum states, qubits, superposition, entanglement, and measurement. We then review the key mathematical tools required—linear algebra, probability theory, and complex numbers—which together form the language of quantum theory.

## Quantum States, Qubits, and Superposition

At the heart of quantum mechanics is the **quantum state**, which encapsulates all the information about a system. In classical physics, a system's state might be described by a set of definite properties, like position and momentum. However, in quantum mechanics, the state is represented by a vector in a complex vector space known as a **Hilbert space**.

Qubits: The Quantum Bit

- **Definition:**
  A **qubit** is the fundamental unit of quantum information. Unlike a classical bit that can only be in one of two states—0 or 1—a qubit can exist in a

continuum of states thanks to the principle of **superposition**.

- **Representation:**

   A qubit is commonly represented as a linear combination of two basis states, usually denoted as $|0\rangle$ and $|1\rangle$. Mathematically, a qubit state $|\psi\rangle$ can be written as:

   $$|\psi\rangle = \alpha|0\rangle + \beta|1\rangle$$

   where $\alpha$ and $\beta$ are complex numbers called probability amplitudes. These amplitudes satisfy the normalization condition:

   $$|\alpha|^2 + |\beta|^2 = 1$$

   This normalization ensures that the total probability of measuring the qubit in one of its basis states is 100%.

Superposition

- **Concept:**

   Superposition is the principle that a quantum system can exist in multiple states simultaneously. In the context of a qubit, this means that it is not just in the state $|0\rangle$ or $|1\rangle$, but in a blend of both. The outcome of a measurement depends on the magnitudes (and phases) of the probability amplitudes $\alpha$ and $\beta$.

- **Implication:**

   Superposition enables quantum computers to process a vast number of possibilities concurrently. For instance, if you have a register of multiple qubits, the overall state is a superposition of all possible combinations of the individual qubits. This exponential growth in state space is what gives quantum algorithms their potential power over classical ones.

# Entanglement and Measurement

Quantum mechanics introduces correlations that have no classical counterpart. **Entanglement** is one of the most striking examples.

Entanglement

- **Definition:**
  When two or more qubits become entangled, their quantum states are no longer independent. Instead, the state of each qubit cannot be described separately from the state of the others—even if they are separated by large distances.

- **Example:**
  Consider two qubits in the entangled Bell state:
  $$|\Phi^+\rangle = \frac{1}{\sqrt{2}} \left( |00\rangle + |11\rangle \right)$$
  In this state, if you measure the first qubit and find it in the state $|0\rangle$, the second qubit will instantaneously be found in $|0\rangle$, and similarly for $|1\rangle$. The outcomes are perfectly correlated despite the absence of a classical communication channel.

- **Significance:**
  Entanglement is not only a fundamental resource in quantum computing—used in algorithms and protocols such as quantum teleportation and superdense coding—but it also challenges our understanding of locality and reality, as famously highlighted in the Einstein-Podolsky-Rosen paradox and Bell's theorem.

Measurement

- **Quantum Measurement:**
  Measurement in quantum mechanics is an active process that fundamentally alters the system. When you measure a qubit, the superposition collapses to one of the basis states. For the qubit $|\psi\rangle$ given by:

$|\psi\rangle = \alpha|0\rangle + \beta|1\rangle,$ the probability of obtaining the result $|0\rangle$ is $|\alpha|^2$ and the probability of obtaining $|1\rangle$ is $|\beta|^2$.

- **Collapse of the Wave Function:**
  This collapse is non-deterministic and highlights the intrinsic probabilistic nature of quantum mechanics. It is not that the system was in a definite state before measurement, but rather that the act of measurement forces the system to 'choose' one of the possible outcomes.

- **Observable and Operators:**
  In quantum mechanics, physical quantities (observables) such as position, momentum, and spin are represented by operators. Measurement involves applying these operators to the quantum state, and the eigenvalues of these operators correspond to the possible outcomes of the measurement.

## Mathematical Foundations: Linear Algebra, Probability, and Complex Numbers

Quantum mechanics is formulated in the language of mathematics, particularly drawing upon linear algebra, probability theory, and complex numbers.

Linear Algebra

- **Hilbert Spaces:**
  A Hilbert space is a complete vector space equipped with an inner product. Quantum states are vectors in this space. For a qubit, the state space is a two-dimensional complex vector space.

- **Vectors and Basis States:**
  States like $|0\rangle$ and $|1\rangle$ form an orthonormal basis for a qubit's Hilbert space. Any state of the qubit can be represented as a linear combination of these

basis states.

- **Operators and Matrices:**
  Operators in quantum mechanics are often represented by matrices. For example, quantum gates that act on qubits are unitary matrices (i.e., matrices U satisfying $U^\dagger U = I$), which ensure that the transformation preserves the normalization of the quantum state.

- **Eigenvalues and Eigenvectors:**
  The outcomes of measurements are associated with the eigenvalues of the operator corresponding to an observable. The quantum state "collapses" to the eigenvector associated with the observed eigenvalue upon measurement.

Probability Theory

- **Probability Amplitudes:**
  The complex numbers $\alpha$ and $\beta$ in a qubit's state represent probability amplitudes. The probability of measuring a particular state is given by the squared magnitude of its amplitude, which introduces a probabilistic framework at the very core of quantum mechanics.

- **Normalization:**
  The condition $|\alpha|^2 + |\beta|^2 = 1$ ensures that the total probability of all possible outcomes sums to one, aligning quantum mechanics with classical probability theory.

- **Statistical Interpretation:**
  Repeated measurements of identically prepared quantum systems allow for the determination of probabilities, linking the abstract quantum formalism with empirical observations.

Complex Numbers

- **Role in Quantum Mechanics:**
  Complex numbers are essential in quantum mechanics. The state vectors, operators, and probability amplitudes are all complex-valued. This inclusion of complex numbers introduces a richer structure than real numbers alone can provide.

- **Phases and Interference:**
  The phase of a complex number (its angle in the complex plane) plays a critical role in quantum interference. When combining probability amplitudes, the relative phases determine whether contributions reinforce or cancel out—crucial for phenomena like interference patterns in the double-slit experiment.

- **Complex Conjugation and Hermitian Operators:**
  Hermitian operators, which represent observable quantities, are equal to their own complex conjugate transpose. This property guarantees that their eigenvalues are real—a necessary condition for physical measurements.

Fundamentally, quantum mechanics replaces deterministic classical descriptions with a probabilistic framework based on quantum states—vectors in a complex Hilbert space. Qubits serve as the basic units of quantum information, capable of existing in superpositions, which exponentially increases the state space when multiple qubits are entangled. Entanglement and measurement introduce deep, non-classical correlations and probabilistic outcomes, leading to groundbreaking phenomena that are being harnessed in quantum computing.

This chapter has provided an extensive overview of the essential concepts:

- **Quantum states, qubits, and superposition** introduce the revolutionary idea that information can be encoded in states that are not strictly binary.

- **Entanglement and measurement** reveal how quantum systems can exhibit correlations beyond classical understanding and how the act of measurement determines observable outcomes.

- **Mathematical foundations** ensure that the complex behavior of quantum systems is rigorously described using the robust tools of linear algebra, probability theory, and complex numbers.

Together, these foundations set the stage for a deeper exploration into quantum circuits, algorithms, and eventually the integration of quantum computing principles with modern cross-platform application development using frameworks like .NET MAUI.

# Quantum Circuits and Key Algorithms

Quantum circuits serve as the backbone of quantum computing, providing a framework in which quantum information is processed through a sequence of operations. In this section, we explore the building blocks of quantum computation—quantum gates and circuit models—delve into the quantum Fourier transform (QFT) and its transformative role in quantum algorithms, and then examine how classical problems are reimagined and solved more efficiently using quantum techniques, specifically through the Deutsch–Jozsa, Grover's, and Shor's algorithms.

## Quantum Gates and Circuit Models

Quantum computation is largely modeled as a series of operations (or "gates") acting on quantum bits (qubits). Just as classical logic circuits use logic gates (like AND, OR, NOT) to process binary information, quantum circuits use quantum gates to manipulate qubits.

Key Quantum Gates

- **Pauli Gates (X, Y, Z):**
  These are the quantum analogs of classical NOT and other bit-flip operations.

- ○ **X gate (bit-flip):** Transforms $|0\rangle$ to $|1\rangle$ and vice versa.

- ○ **Y gate:** Combines bit and phase flip.

- ○ **Z gate (phase flip):** Leaves $|0\rangle$ unchanged and flips the sign of $|1\rangle$.

- **Hadamard Gate (H):**
  Creates superposition by transforming a basis state into an equal superposition of $|0\rangle$ and $|1\rangle$. For example,
  H|0⟩=12(|0⟩+|1⟩))H|0\rangle = \frac{1}{\sqrt{2}}(|0\rangle + |1\rangle)
  This gate is critical for initializing qubits into states that can interfere constructively or destructively later in the algorithm.

- **Controlled Gates (e.g., CNOT):**
  Controlled operations perform a gate operation on a target qubit conditioned on the state of a control qubit.

  - ○ **CNOT (Controlled-NOT):** Flips the target qubit if the control qubit is $|1\rangle$. It is essential for creating entanglement between qubits.

- **Phase Gates (S, T):**
  Introduce specific phase shifts to quantum states, which can be crucial for fine-tuning interference effects in quantum algorithms.

- **Swap Gate:**
  Exchanges the states of two qubits, useful in routing qubits within a quantum circuit.

Quantum Circuit Model

A quantum circuit is essentially a diagrammatic representation that shows the flow of qubits through a sequence of quantum gates:

- **Structure:**
  Each horizontal line in a quantum circuit represents a qubit, and vertical

lines (or boxes) indicate the application of gates at specific time steps. The overall circuit represents the unitary transformation that is applied to the initial quantum state.

- **Execution:**
  The computation begins with an initial state—often a product state of qubits in $|0\rangle$ or a specific superposition—and proceeds by sequentially applying the defined gates. Finally, measurements are performed on the qubits, collapsing their states to yield classical output.

- **Universality:**
  A set of quantum gates is said to be universal if any unitary operation (and thus any quantum computation) can be approximated to arbitrary precision by a circuit composed solely of those gates. The combination of the Hadamard gate, CNOT, and a suitable phase gate (like the T gate) forms a universal set for quantum computation.

The quantum circuit model encapsulates the operational idea behind quantum computers. By chaining together simple gates, complex algorithms can be built that leverage the principles of superposition and entanglement to perform computations beyond classical capabilities.

## The Quantum Fourier Transform (QFT)

The Quantum Fourier Transform (QFT) is a quantum analogue of the classical discrete Fourier transform (DFT) but is executed exponentially faster on a quantum computer. The QFT transforms a quantum state from the computational basis into a frequency domain, a change of basis that is essential in many quantum algorithms.

Core Concepts of QFT

- **Mathematical Definition:**
  For an nn-qubit system (where $N=2nN = 2\textasciicircum n$), the QFT maps a basis state

$|x\rangle$|x\rangle to:

QFT($|x\rangle$)=1N∑y=0N−1e2πi xy/N|y⟩\text{QFT}(|x\rangle) = \frac{1}{\sqrt{N}} \sum_{y=0}^{N-1} e^{2\pi i \, xy/N} |y\rangle

Here, xx and yy are integers between 0 and N−1N-1. The transformation is unitary, preserving the overall probability amplitude.

- **Efficiency:**
  Classical DFTs typically require O(NlogN)O(N \log N) operations (using algorithms like the Fast Fourier Transform). In contrast, the QFT can be implemented using O(n2)O(n^2) quantum gates, which is exponentially faster in terms of the number of qubits nn.

- **Implementation:**
  The QFT is constructed using a sequence of Hadamard and controlled phase shift gates. Its circuit structure is highly regular, making it amenable to efficient quantum circuit design.

Applications of QFT

- **Period Finding:**
  The QFT is a cornerstone of Shor's algorithm, where it is used to determine the period of a function—a crucial step in factoring large integers.

- **Phase Estimation:**
  In many quantum algorithms, estimating the phase (or eigenvalue) corresponding to an eigenstate of a unitary operator is essential. The QFT provides the mechanism to extract this information.

- **Signal Processing:**
  Just as the classical Fourier transform is used in signal processing, the QFT can process and analyze quantum information encoded in frequency domains, which has implications in quantum simulations and error correction.

# Classical Algorithms Reimagined for Quantum Computation

Quantum computing introduces novel approaches to solving problems that are intractable or less efficient on classical computers. Let's examine three pivotal algorithms that exemplify this shift.

Deutsch–Jozsa Algorithm

- **Problem Statement:**
  The Deutsch–Jozsa problem asks whether a given Boolean function $f:\{0,1\}n \rightarrow \{0,1\} f: \backslash\{0,1\backslash\}^n \backslash rightarrow \backslash\{0,1\backslash\}$ is constant (the same output for all inputs) or balanced (outputs 0 for exactly half of the inputs and 1 for the other half). Classically, in the worst case, $2n-1+12^{n-1} + 1$ evaluations of ff are needed to determine this with certainty.

- **Quantum Advantage:**
  The Deutsch–Jozsa algorithm solves this problem with just a single evaluation (query) of ff by exploiting superposition and interference.

  - **Procedure:**

    1. Prepare an nn-qubit register in superposition using Hadamard gates.

    2. Apply the oracle UfU_f that encodes the function.

    3. Use another round of Hadamard transforms and then measure.

  - **Outcome:**
    The measurement yields a result that immediately distinguishes between the constant and balanced cases.

- **Significance:**
  Although the problem is contrived and not of practical use by itself, the

algorithm demonstrates the potential for quantum parallelism and interference to achieve exponential speedup in specific tasks.

## Grover's Search Algorithm

- **Problem Statement:**
  Grover's algorithm addresses the unstructured search problem: given an unsorted database of $N$ items, find a marked item. Classically, this requires $O(N)$ queries, while Grover's algorithm provides a quadratic speedup.

- **Quantum Mechanism:**
  Grover's algorithm uses the concept of amplitude amplification:

  - **Initialization:**
    All states are initialized into an equal superposition using Hadamard gates.

  - **Oracle and Diffusion Operator:**
    The algorithm alternates between an oracle that inverts the phase of the target state and a diffusion operator (inversion about the mean) that amplifies the probability amplitude of the marked state.

  - **Iterations:**
    Repeating these steps approximately $O(\sqrt{N})$ times increases the likelihood of measuring the marked state.

- **Outcome and Impact:**
  Although it provides only a quadratic speedup (as opposed to exponential), Grover's algorithm is widely applicable to various search and optimization problems, making it one of the most celebrated quantum algorithms.

Shor's Algorithm

- **Problem Statement:**
  Shor's algorithm efficiently factors large composite numbers and computes discrete logarithms—problems that underpin the security of many classical cryptographic schemes. Classically, the best-known factoring algorithms run in sub-exponential time, but Shor's algorithm runs in polynomial time.

- **Quantum Procedure:**
  The algorithm combines quantum and classical techniques:

  - **Period Finding:**
    The core quantum part of Shor's algorithm is used to find the period rr of the function $f(x)=a x \mod N$ $f(x) = a^x \mod N$. This is achieved by preparing a superposition, applying modular exponentiation, and then performing the quantum Fourier transform (QFT) to extract the periodicity.

  - **Classical Post-Processing:**
    Once the period rr is determined, classical algorithms are used to compute the greatest common divisor (GCD) and ultimately derive the factors of the number NN.

- **Significance:**
  Shor's algorithm is perhaps the most famous example of quantum computing's potential to disrupt current cryptographic systems, as it shows that quantum computers could, in principle, break RSA encryption.


Quantum circuits offer a powerful and elegant way to represent quantum computations, where a sequence of quantum gates manipulates qubits to perform complex operations. The quantum Fourier transform stands out as a transformative tool that enables many quantum algorithms to operate with exponential speedups over their classical counterparts.

By reimagining classical algorithms through the lens of quantum mechanics—exemplified by the Deutsch–Jozsa, Grover's, and Shor's algorithms—quantum computing demonstrates its potential to solve problems more efficiently than traditional computers. These algorithms harness core quantum phenomena like superposition, interference, and entanglement to create new paradigms for computation, paving the way for breakthroughs in cryptography, optimization, and beyond.

This section provides the necessary theoretical and practical foundation for the subsequent parts of the book, where we will explore more advanced quantum circuits, delve into error correction, and ultimately integrate these quantum techniques into cross-platform applications using modern frameworks like .NET MAUI.

# Quantum Error Correction and Noise Management

Quantum systems are inherently fragile. Unlike classical bits, which can be duplicated and protected using traditional error-correcting techniques, quantum bits (qubits) are susceptible to errors from a variety of sources due to their delicate nature. As a result, the field of quantum error correction (QEC) is a critical area of research that ensures reliable quantum computation in the presence of noise. In this section, we explore the sources and types of quantum noise, delve into the theory behind error-correcting codes and threshold theorems, and discuss strategies for robust quantum computation.

## Sources and Types of Quantum Noise

Quantum noise arises from interactions between the quantum system and its surrounding environment. These interactions can disturb the qubits in unpredictable ways, leading to errors in the stored or processed information. Some of the primary sources and types of quantum noise include:

- **Decoherence:**
  Decoherence is the process by which a quantum system loses its quantum properties as it interacts with its environment. This phenomenon results in the decay of superposition states into classical mixtures, effectively "destroying" the delicate interference patterns that are central to quantum

computation.

- **Bit-Flip and Phase-Flip Errors:**

  - **Bit-flip errors:** Analogous to classical bit errors, where a qubit in state $|0\rangle$ flips to $|1\rangle$, and vice versa. This error can be modeled by the Pauli-X operator.

  - **Phase-flip errors:** Here, the phase of the qubit is inverted, meaning that $|1\rangle$ gains a minus sign relative to $|0\rangle$. The Pauli-Z operator describes this effect.

  - **Combined errors:** Often, errors can be a combination of bit and phase flips, represented by the Pauli-Y operator (which combines the effects of X and Z up to a phase factor).

- **Depolarizing Noise:**
  This model represents a scenario where a qubit is replaced with a completely mixed state with a certain probability. Depolarizing noise can be viewed as a combination of bit-flip, phase-flip, and both errors simultaneously, and it is often used to model general noise in quantum channels.

- **Amplitude Damping:**
  Amplitude damping errors occur when energy dissipates from a qubit to its environment. For instance, in a system where qubits are implemented with two-level atoms or superconducting circuits, the excited state may decay to the ground state over time, leading to a loss of quantum information.

- **Phase Damping:**
  Phase damping refers to errors that specifically cause loss of phase coherence between quantum states without an exchange of energy. This form of noise is particularly relevant in optical systems and is a primary contributor to decoherence.

Understanding these noise sources is crucial for designing error correction schemes. Each type of noise may require different strategies to detect and correct errors without disturbing the quantum information more than necessary.

## Error-Correcting Codes and Threshold Theorems

Quantum error-correcting codes are designed to protect quantum information against errors introduced by various noise sources. They work by encoding the logical state of a qubit into a larger Hilbert space spanned by multiple physical qubits. This redundancy enables the detection and correction of errors without directly measuring and thereby disturbing the encoded quantum state.

Key Concepts in Quantum Error Correction

- **Encoding and Redundancy:**
  Quantum information is encoded across multiple physical qubits. For example, a single logical qubit might be represented by a highly entangled state of several physical qubits. Popular codes include:

  - **Shor Code:** Encodes one logical qubit into nine physical qubits, correcting arbitrary single-qubit errors.

  - **Steane Code:** A seven-qubit code that corrects single-qubit errors by exploiting the structure of classical linear codes.

  - **Surface Codes:** These codes use a two-dimensional lattice of qubits and have gained prominence due to their relatively high error thresholds and suitability for scalable implementations.

- **Syndrome Measurement:**
  Instead of directly measuring the quantum state (which would collapse the superposition), syndrome measurements extract information about the error without revealing the encoded logical state. The measurement results (syndromes) indicate which error, if any, has occurred, allowing for targeted

recovery operations.

- **Error-Correction Conditions:**
  To successfully correct errors, a quantum code must satisfy specific conditions. These conditions ensure that different error operators map the encoded state into orthogonal subspaces, so that each error syndrome uniquely identifies the error type.

Threshold Theorems

A key result in quantum error correction is the **threshold theorem**, which states that if the error rate per physical qubit is below a certain threshold, fault-tolerant quantum computation becomes feasible. This means that errors can be corrected faster than they accumulate, allowing for arbitrarily long quantum computations provided the error rates are sufficiently low.

- **Fault-Tolerance:**
  Fault-tolerant quantum computation refers to the construction of quantum circuits that continue to operate correctly even when some components fail. By carefully designing circuits and using error-correcting codes, errors can be contained and corrected at every step of the computation.

- **Error Threshold:**
  The error threshold is a critical value. If the error probability per gate or per qubit is below this threshold, the overall error rate of the computation can be suppressed through recursive error correction and concatenated codes. Various architectures (such as surface codes) have demonstrated thresholds on the order of 1% or higher in some experimental setups.

The threshold theorem is fundamental because it provides a roadmap for building scalable quantum computers: as long as the physical implementation maintains error rates below the threshold, logical errors can be managed, and reliable computation can be achieved.

# Strategies for Robust Quantum Computation

Given the inevitability of noise in quantum systems, multiple strategies are being pursued to ensure robust quantum computation:

- **Concatenated Codes:**
  In concatenated coding, a quantum code is applied recursively. Each logical qubit is encoded into several physical qubits using one error-correcting code, and then those logical qubits are themselves encoded using another layer of coding. This hierarchical approach can dramatically reduce the effective error rate.

- **Surface Codes and Topological Quantum Error Correction:**
  Surface codes use a two-dimensional grid of qubits where error correction is implemented by measuring stabilizers associated with local regions of the grid. Their high error thresholds and local connectivity requirements make them particularly attractive for practical implementations in solid-state and superconducting qubit systems.

- **Fault-Tolerant Gate Construction:**
  Constructing gates in a fault-tolerant manner ensures that errors during gate operations do not propagate uncontrollably through the quantum circuit. Techniques such as transversal gates (where each physical qubit in a logical qubit is operated on independently) are crucial in this regard.

- **Error Mitigation Techniques:**
  For near-term quantum devices (NISQ-era devices), full fault tolerance may not be achievable. Instead, error mitigation techniques—such as extrapolating error rates, using symmetry verification, and optimizing control pulses—are employed to reduce the impact of noise without full-scale error correction.

- **Dynamic Decoupling and Noise Tailoring:**
  Dynamic decoupling involves applying a sequence of pulses to the qubits to average out environmental noise, much like spinning a top can stabilize its orientation. Additionally, engineering the qubit environment and material properties can tailor the noise characteristics, making them more amenable to error correction.

- **Hybrid Quantum-Classical Approaches:**
  In many practical applications, quantum computers will work in tandem with classical processors. Hybrid algorithms, such as the variational quantum eigensolver (VQE) or quantum approximate optimization algorithm (QAOA), use the quantum processor for tasks where it has an advantage while relying on classical optimization routines to fine-tune parameters. These approaches are inherently more robust against noise because they can tolerate a degree of imperfection in quantum computations.

Quantum error correction and noise management are at the heart of reliable quantum computation. The diverse sources of quantum noise—from decoherence and bit-flip/phase-flip errors to amplitude damping and depolarization—pose significant challenges. To counteract these errors, quantum error-correcting codes, such as the Shor, Steane, and surface codes, use redundancy and syndrome measurements to detect and correct errors without collapsing the quantum state. The threshold theorem offers hope by showing that, provided the error rates are below a critical threshold, fault-tolerant computation is achievable through hierarchical (concatenated) error correction and other robust strategies.

Together, these techniques and strategies pave the way for robust quantum computation, ensuring that as we scale quantum systems, we can effectively manage and mitigate errors. This lays the foundation for building practical, reliable quantum computers that can eventually outperform classical systems on a range of computational tasks.

In the following sections of this book, we will build on these concepts to explore the design of quantum circuits and further integrate quantum computation principles into modern application frameworks like .NET MAUI, ultimately bridging the gap between quantum theory and real-world software development.

# Quantum Information Theory and Cryptography

Quantum information theory extends classical concepts of information into the quantum domain, offering a framework to quantify and manipulate information encoded in quantum states. Simultaneously, quantum cryptography harnesses unique quantum phenomena to secure communications in ways that are provably secure against both classical and quantum adversaries. In this section, we explore three key areas:

1. **Entropy, Information Measures, and Quantum Channels**

2. **Quantum Key Distribution and Cryptographic Protocols**

3. **Security Implications of Quantum Computing**

## Entropy, Information Measures, and Quantum Channels

Quantum Entropy and Information Measures

In classical information theory, entropy quantifies the uncertainty or randomness in a probability distribution. In the quantum realm, similar concepts exist to characterize the uncertainty of quantum states.

- **Von Neumann Entropy:**
  The von Neumann entropy $S(\rho)$ of a quantum state, described by a density matrix $\rho$, is defined as:
  $$S(\rho) = -\mathrm{Tr}(\rho \log \rho)$$
  This measure captures the uncertainty inherent in a quantum state. Pure states have zero entropy (complete information), whereas mixed states (statistical ensembles of pure states) have nonzero entropy, reflecting classical randomness introduced by decoherence or imperfect preparation.

- **Conditional and Mutual Quantum Information:**

  - **Conditional Entropy:**
    For a bipartite quantum state $\rho_{AB}$, the conditional entropy $S(A|B)$ is given by:
    $$S(A|B) = S(\rho_{AB}) - S(\rho_B)$$
    Interestingly, unlike its classical counterpart, quantum conditional entropy can be negative—a phenomenon associated with entanglement.

  - **Mutual Information:**
    The mutual information quantifies the total correlations between two quantum systems:
    $$I(A:B) = S(\rho_A) + S(\rho_B) - S(\rho_{AB})$$
    It measures how much information is shared between systems $A$ and $B$.

- **Relative Entropy and Fidelity:**
  Other useful measures include the quantum relative entropy, which compares two states, and fidelity, which quantifies the closeness between quantum states. These metrics are essential for tasks such as quantum hypothesis testing and the evaluation of quantum communication protocols.

Quantum Channels

A quantum channel represents the physical or abstract process by which quantum information is transmitted or transformed. Mathematically, quantum channels are completely positive, trace-preserving (CPTP) maps acting on density matrices.

- **Channel Capacity:**
  The capacity of a quantum channel defines the maximum rate at which quantum information can be reliably transmitted. There are various capacities—quantum capacity (for transmitting quantum states), classical capacity (for classical information), and private capacity (for secure information transmission).

- **Noisy Quantum Channels:**
  In reality, all quantum channels are subject to noise, which can be modeled using various error processes (e.g., depolarizing channels, amplitude damping channels). Quantum error correction and noise mitigation strategies are designed to protect quantum information as it traverses these channels.

- **Channel Coding Theorems:**
  Similar to Shannon's theorems in classical information theory, quantum channel coding theorems provide limits on information transmission. These results guide the development of error-correcting codes that can achieve the theoretical capacities of quantum channels.

## Quantum Key Distribution and Cryptographic Protocols

Quantum cryptography leverages the principles of quantum mechanics to secure communications. Unlike classical cryptographic methods that rely on computational hardness assumptions, quantum cryptographic protocols can offer unconditional security based on physical laws.

Quantum Key Distribution (QKD)

- **Fundamental Principle:**
  QKD enables two parties (commonly referred to as Alice and Bob) to establish a shared, secret key. The security of QKD arises from the no-cloning theorem and the fact that measurement in quantum mechanics disturbs the state. Any eavesdropper (Eve) attempting to intercept the key will inevitably introduce detectable anomalies.

- **Key Protocols:**

  - **BB84 Protocol:**
    The first and most famous QKD protocol, BB84, uses two sets of conjugate bases (e.g., rectilinear and diagonal polarization states of photons). Alice sends qubits prepared in one of these bases, and Bob measures them in randomly chosen bases. After the quantum transmission, they publicly compare basis choices (but not outcomes) to establish a key, while any discrepancy signals eavesdropping.

  - **E91 Protocol:**
    Based on entanglement, the E91 protocol uses pairs of entangled particles shared between Alice and Bob. Measurement correlations between entangled pairs are used to generate a key, with the security guarantee rooted in Bell's theorem.

  - **B92 Protocol:**
    A simplified version of BB84, the B92 protocol uses only two non-orthogonal quantum states. Its security derives from the fact that non-orthogonal states cannot be perfectly distinguished, ensuring that eavesdropping will introduce errors.

Other Cryptographic Protocols

- **Quantum Secure Direct Communication (QSDC):**
  Instead of establishing a shared key, QSDC allows for the direct

transmission of confidential messages using quantum states.

- **Quantum Authentication:**
  Protocols for quantum authentication ensure that the origin and integrity of quantum messages are verified, preventing impersonation and tampering.

- **Privacy Amplification and Information Reconciliation:**
  In realistic scenarios, some errors and information leakage might occur during the key distribution process. Privacy amplification techniques reduce Eve's knowledge of the key, while information reconciliation ensures that Alice and Bob have identical keys despite the presence of noise.

# Security Implications of Quantum Computing

Quantum computing is set to have a profound impact on information security, both by enhancing cryptographic methods and by threatening the security of classical cryptosystems.

Threats to Classical Cryptography

- **Shor's Algorithm:**
  Perhaps the most significant security implication is Shor's algorithm, which can efficiently factor large composite numbers and compute discrete logarithms. Since many classical cryptosystems (e.g., RSA, ECC) rely on the intractability of these problems, a sufficiently powerful quantum computer could potentially break these systems.

- **Post-Quantum Cryptography:**
  In response, researchers are developing cryptographic algorithms believed to be secure against quantum attacks. These algorithms, based on lattice problems, code-based cryptography, and multivariate quadratic equations, are collectively known as post-quantum or quantum-resistant cryptography.

Opportunities for Enhanced Security

- **Quantum Key Distribution (QKD):**
  QKD provides an intrinsically secure method for key distribution that is not based on computational assumptions. The fundamental principles of quantum mechanics guarantee that any eavesdropping attempt will be detected, providing a level of security that is provably unconditional.

- **Quantum Random Number Generation:**
  Quantum processes can generate truly random numbers, which are essential for secure cryptographic systems. This randomness improves the security of cryptographic keys and protocols.

- **Device-Independent Cryptography:**
  Advances in quantum cryptography are paving the way for device-independent protocols. These protocols can ensure security even when the devices used are untrusted or imperfect, relying solely on the violation of Bell inequalities to guarantee security.

Challenges and Future Directions

- **Practical Implementation:**
  While theoretical models of quantum cryptography offer high levels of security, practical implementations must contend with losses, noise, and imperfect detectors. Bridging this gap requires continued research in quantum error correction, advanced materials, and system design.

- **Integration with Existing Infrastructure:**
  For quantum cryptographic systems to be widely adopted, they must be integrated with existing communication networks. This involves addressing challenges in scalability, cost, and interoperability with classical systems.

- **Regulatory and Standardization Issues:**
  As quantum technologies mature, there will be a need for standards and regulatory frameworks to govern their use in cryptography and secure

communications. International collaboration will be key to ensuring global security in the quantum era.

Quantum information theory and cryptography represent a paradigm shift in how we conceive, measure, and secure information. By extending classical information measures into the quantum realm through tools like the von Neumann entropy and mutual information, we gain a deeper understanding of quantum channels and the limits of information transfer.

Quantum key distribution protocols—most notably BB84, E91, and B92—leverage the fundamental properties of quantum mechanics to offer security guarantees that are immune to both classical and quantum computational attacks. At the same time, the advent of quantum computing poses significant risks to conventional cryptographic systems, spurring the development of post-quantum cryptography to safeguard future communications.

The interplay between quantum information theory and cryptography not only deepens our theoretical understanding of quantum mechanics but also provides practical solutions for secure communication in an increasingly connected and data-driven world. As quantum technologies continue to evolve, the integration of these principles into secure systems will be paramount in maintaining the confidentiality, integrity, and authenticity of information in the quantum era.

In the subsequent chapters, we will build on these foundations to explore how quantum algorithms, error correction, and robust circuit designs come together to make quantum computing a practical reality—and how these advancements can be integrated into modern, cross-platform applications using frameworks such as .NET MAUI.

# Programming Quantum Computers

Programming quantum computers requires a shift in mindset from classical programming, as quantum algorithms operate on principles like superposition and entanglement. This section explores the ecosystem of quantum programming languages and frameworks, the available simulation and cloud-based computing services, and best practices to design and implement robust quantum algorithms.

## Overview of Quantum Programming Languages and Frameworks

Several quantum programming languages and software frameworks have emerged to help developers design, simulate, and eventually run quantum algorithms on real quantum hardware. These tools abstract much of the underlying quantum mechanical complexity, enabling researchers and developers to focus on algorithm design. Key players include:

- **Q#:**
  Developed by Microsoft as part of the Quantum Development Kit, Q# is a domain-specific language tailored for quantum programming. It integrates with Visual Studio and Visual Studio Code, and it supports classical host programs written in C# or Python. Q# provides a rich library of quantum

operations and functions, facilitating the design of quantum algorithms such as the quantum Fourier transform, Grover's search, and more.

- **Qiskit:**
  An open-source quantum computing framework from IBM, Qiskit allows developers to write quantum programs in Python. Qiskit's modular design consists of several components:

  - **Terra:** Provides the foundation for quantum circuit creation and manipulation.

  - **Aer:** Offers high-performance simulators for testing quantum circuits.

  - **Ignis:** Focuses on quantum error mitigation and noise characterization.

  - **Aqua:** Contains high-level applications for quantum chemistry, optimization, and machine learning.
    With Qiskit, users can run experiments on IBM's cloud-based quantum processors, bridging the gap between simulation and real quantum hardware.

- **Cirq:**
  Developed by Google, Cirq is a Python library designed for creating, editing, and invoking noisy intermediate-scale quantum (NISQ) circuits. Cirq is optimized for near-term quantum devices and supports the design of circuits that can be executed on quantum processors like those available through the Google Quantum AI platform. Its focus is on simplicity and flexibility, allowing researchers to experiment with quantum circuits and integrate them into hybrid quantum-classical workflows.

- **Other Frameworks:**
  Beyond these three, several other frameworks and languages are emerging or evolving:

- **PyQuil:** A Python library developed by Rigetti Computing, designed to program Rigetti's quantum processors via the Forest platform.

- **Ocean:** D-Wave's suite for quantum annealing, focusing on optimization problems.

- **Strange:** A Java-based quantum computing simulator aimed at helping developers get hands-on experience with quantum programming using a familiar language.

Each language and framework has its own strengths, often shaped by the type of quantum hardware they target (gate-based versus annealing) and their integration with classical programming environments. The choice of tool often depends on the specific research problem, available hardware, and personal or organizational preferences.

## Simulators and Cloud-Based Quantum Computing Services

While fully error-corrected quantum hardware is still under development, robust simulators and cloud-based quantum computing services allow developers to experiment with quantum algorithms today.

- **Quantum Simulators:**
  Simulators are software tools that mimic the behavior of quantum computers. They are essential for testing and debugging quantum circuits before deployment on actual hardware. Common simulators include:

  - **Qiskit Aer:** A high-performance simulator that can emulate quantum circuits with noise models. It is particularly useful for experimenting with various error models and benchmarking algorithms.

  - **Cirq Simulator:** Google's Cirq framework includes simulators capable of handling noisy, intermediate-scale quantum (NISQ) circuits.

- **Rigetti's QVM (Quantum Virtual Machine):** Part of the Forest platform, QVM allows users to simulate circuits written in PyQuil.

- **Microsoft's Quantum Simulator:** Integrated within the Quantum Development Kit, it supports Q# programs and provides debugging and visualization tools.

- These simulators vary in scale and performance. While they can accurately model small systems (up to 30–40 qubits in some cases), simulating larger quantum systems remains challenging due to the exponential growth of the quantum state space.

- **Cloud-Based Quantum Computing Services:**
  In addition to simulators, several organizations offer access to real quantum hardware via cloud services:

  - **IBM Quantum Experience:** IBM's cloud service provides access to a range of quantum processors. Users can design and run quantum circuits using Qiskit, access real hardware, and participate in community challenges.

  - **Microsoft Azure Quantum:** This platform offers access to quantum hardware from multiple providers along with the Q# language and associated development tools.

  - **Amazon Braket:** A fully managed quantum computing service that provides access to quantum hardware from various vendors along with integrated simulators.

  - **Rigetti Computing's Quantum Cloud Services (QCS):** Rigetti offers cloud access to its quantum processors and associated software tools via the Forest platform.

- These services democratize access to quantum computing by removing the need for expensive local hardware, enabling researchers and developers worldwide to run experiments on state-of-the-art quantum devices.

## Coding Best Practices for Quantum Algorithms

Quantum programming, while conceptually different from classical programming, also benefits from structured development practices. Here are some best practices for coding quantum algorithms:

- **Modular Circuit Design:**
  Decompose complex quantum algorithms into modular subroutines. This practice, analogous to using functions or classes in classical programming, makes your code more maintainable and reusable. For example, encapsulate the quantum Fourier transform as a separate module that can be integrated into different algorithms.

- **Circuit Optimization:**
  Quantum resources (such as qubit count and gate depth) are limited. Optimize your circuits by:

  - **Reducing gate counts:** Use the minimum number of gates necessary to achieve the desired transformation.

  - **Circuit simplification:** Apply techniques like gate cancellation and commutation rules to simplify your circuit.

  - **Error mitigation:** Integrate error correction or error mitigation strategies where possible to improve the fidelity of your computation.

- **Testing and Simulation:**
  Before deploying algorithms on real quantum hardware, rigorously test your

circuits using simulators. This includes:

- ○ **Unit testing:** Write unit tests for individual subroutines or quantum operations.

- ○ **Noise modeling:** Use simulators that include noise to evaluate the robustness of your algorithm against realistic imperfections.

- ○ **Benchmarking:** Compare the performance of your quantum algorithm on simulators against classical counterparts where applicable.

- **Hybrid Approaches:**
 Leverage hybrid quantum-classical algorithms, such as variational quantum eigensolvers (VQE) or the quantum approximate optimization algorithm (QAOA). These approaches use the quantum computer for tasks where it provides an advantage while relying on classical optimization to fine-tune parameters, making them more resilient to noise.

- **Documentation and Code Clarity:**
 Quantum code can be non-intuitive, so thorough documentation is crucial. Explain the purpose of each quantum subroutine, the expected input/output, and any assumptions made. Comments, flow diagrams, and annotated circuit diagrams can help others (and your future self) understand and maintain the code.

- **Version Control and Reproducibility:**
 Use version control systems (like Git) to track changes and ensure reproducibility of quantum experiments. Document the simulation environment, dependencies, and hardware settings to allow others to replicate your results.

- **Continuous Learning and Community Engagement:**
 Quantum programming is an evolving field. Stay updated with the latest developments in quantum hardware, algorithms, and software tools by

engaging with the quantum computing community. Contributing to open-source projects, participating in hackathons, and attending workshops can provide valuable insights and foster collaboration.

Programming quantum computers combines the challenges of classical software development with the unique demands of quantum mechanics. The ecosystem of quantum programming languages—such as Q#, Qiskit, Cirq, and others—provides diverse tools for designing and simulating quantum circuits, while cloud-based services offer real hardware access to test and run algorithms. By following best practices in modular design, circuit optimization, testing, documentation, and community engagement, developers can build robust and efficient quantum algorithms.

This integrated approach not only accelerates research and innovation in quantum computing but also paves the way for practical applications that leverage quantum advantages in fields ranging from cryptography to optimization and beyond. In the upcoming sections, we will build on these principles to explore the integration of quantum computation with modern cross-platform frameworks, ultimately bridging the gap between quantum theory and real-world application development.

# Building a Quantum Simulator Application with .NET MAUI

## Introduction to .NET MAUI and Its Relevance for App Development

What is .NET MAUI?

.NET Multi-platform App UI (MAUI) is a cross-platform framework developed by Microsoft that enables developers to build applications that run seamlessly on **Windows, macOS, iOS, and Android** using a **single codebase**. It is the evolution of Xamarin.Forms, providing a modern and unified approach to cross-platform app development.

Why Use .NET MAUI for Quantum Simulator Development?

Building a **quantum simulator** requires a user-friendly interface and efficient computing power. .NET MAUI provides several advantages for this purpose:

1. **Cross-Platform Compatibility**

   ○ Quantum computing research and applications require access across multiple platforms (e.g., desktop, mobile, and tablets). .NET MAUI ensures that the application can run on various devices without needing separate codebases.

2. **Integration with Quantum SDKs**

   o MAUI supports integration with Python-based quantum computing frameworks like **Qiskit**, as well as Microsoft's **Q# and Azure Quantum**, making it ideal for developing quantum applications.

3. **Powerful UI/UX Features**

   o Quantum simulations often require visual representations of **quantum circuits, wavefunctions, and entanglement diagrams**. .NET MAUI provides **native UI rendering** and **graphic capabilities** to build intuitive visual interfaces.

4. **Performance and Scalability**

   o Leveraging .NET's efficiency, a quantum simulator app can perform computational tasks effectively while providing a smooth user experience.

5. **Seamless Cloud Integration**

   o A quantum simulator app may require access to **cloud-based quantum processors**. MAUI supports APIs to connect with **IBM Quantum, Azure Quantum, and Amazon Braket**.

## Setting Up Your Development Environment for Cross-Platform Projects

Before developing the quantum simulator app, ensure your environment is set up correctly.

1. Install .NET SDK and .NET MAUI

To develop a .NET MAUI application, you need the latest **.NET SDK** and **MAUI workloads** installed.

Steps to Install .NET MAUI:

1. **Install .NET SDK**
   Download and install the latest .NET SDK from Microsoft's official website.

**Enable .NET MAUI Workloads**
Open a command prompt or terminal and run:

dotnet workload install maui

2.

**Verify Installation**
Check if MAUI is installed properly:

dotnet --list-sdks

3.

2. Install an IDE (Visual Studio 2022 or VS Code)

.NET MAUI is best supported on **Visual Studio 2022** with the **MAUI workload**. Ensure you enable:

- **.NET MAUI Development**

- **Android/iOS/Mac Catalyst support** (if building for mobile)

- **Windows support (UWP and WinUI)**

3. Configure the Emulator or Physical Device

To test mobile versions of the app, set up an **Android Emulator** or **iOS Simulator**:

- For **Windows**, install **Android SDK and Emulator**.

- For **macOS**, install **Xcode** to support iOS development.

4. Set Up Quantum Libraries

The simulator will rely on **quantum computing libraries** such as:

**Q# and Microsoft Quantum SDK**

dotnet new -i Microsoft.Quantum.ProjectTemplates

- 

**Qiskit (for Python-based quantum simulations)**

pip install qiskit

-

### Cirq (Google's quantum framework)

pip install cirq

- 

### Integration with IBM Quantum Cloud

pip install qiskit-ibm-provider

- 

With the environment ready, we can now move to **project planning**.


## Project Planning: Defining Goals for a Quantum Simulation App

A quantum simulator app aims to **simulate quantum circuits and visualize quantum states** without requiring actual quantum hardware. The project planning stage involves defining core features and designing a user-friendly architecture.

1. Defining the Scope of the Quantum Simulator

The app should provide:

- **Quantum Circuit Builder**: Drag-and-drop interface to create quantum circuits.

- **Quantum Gate Simulations**: Support for Hadamard, Pauli-X, CNOT, and other gates.

- **Quantum State Visualization**: Display Bloch spheres and probability distributions.

- **Quantum Noise Simulation**: Model realistic quantum decoherence.

- **Integration with Qiskit and Q#**: Execute circuits using different quantum frameworks.

- **Cloud-Based Quantum Execution**: Allow users to run experiments on IBM Quantum or Azure Quantum.

2. Choosing the App's Architecture

A clean architecture ensures maintainability and scalability. We can use:

- **MVVM (Model-View-ViewModel) Architecture**

  - **Model**: Quantum simulation logic (e.g., quantum circuit representation).

  - **View**: User interface (interactive circuit editor, result visualizations).

  - **ViewModel**: Business logic connecting UI with quantum computations.

- **Backend Options**:

  - Local simulations using **Qiskit** or **Q#**.

  - Cloud execution via **Azure Quantum** or **IBM Quantum Cloud API**.

3. Designing the UI/UX

A user-friendly interface is critical. **Key UI components** include:

- **Circuit Editor:** A drag-and-drop interface for building quantum circuits.

- **Gate Palette:** Users can choose from a set of quantum gates.

- **State Visualizer:** Graphs and Bloch spheres to represent quantum states.

- **Execution Panel:** Buttons to **simulate, reset, and export** circuits.

- **Results Panel:** Display measurement results and probabilities.

4. Establishing the Development Milestones

A structured development plan ensures efficient progress:

| Phase | Task | Expected Outcome |
| --- | --- | --- |
| **Phase 1** | Setup .NET MAUI project, configure dependencies | Basic app scaffold ready |
| **Phase 2** | Implement UI (Quantum Circuit Builder, Gate Palette) | User can create circuits visually |
| **Phase 3** | Add quantum simulation logic (Qiskit, Q# integration) | Circuits can be simulated locally |
| **Phase 4** | Implement visualization (Bloch sphere, probability graphs) | Users can see quantum state evolution |
| **Phase 5** | Integrate with IBM Quantum/Azure Quantum | Users can run real quantum computations |
| **Phase 6** | Optimize UI/UX and performance | Smooth, efficient app |

| **Phase 7** | Final testing and deployment | App ready for release |

Building a **Quantum Simulator Application with .NET MAUI** combines cutting-edge quantum computing with a modern cross-platform development framework. By leveraging .NET MAUI's robust UI capabilities and integrating quantum frameworks like Qiskit, Cirq, and Q#, we can create a powerful and intuitive quantum computing tool.

In the next section, we will begin implementing the **Quantum Circuit Builder UI**, allowing users to construct quantum circuits interactively.

# .NET MAUI Fundamentals for Quantum Applications

Integrating quantum computing simulations into cross-platform applications requires a robust and flexible UI framework. .NET MAUI (Multi-platform App UI) provides a modern environment for building applications that run seamlessly on Windows, macOS, iOS, and Android. In this section, we delve into the essential elements of .NET MAUI for quantum applications, covering core UI concepts, the implementation of the MVVM design pattern for a clean and maintainable architecture, and techniques for data binding and navigation across multiple platforms.

## Core UI Concepts in .NET MAUI: XAML, Layouts, and Controls

XAML (eXtensible Application Markup Language)

- **Declarative UI Definition:**
  XAML enables developers to define user interfaces in a declarative manner. You describe the layout and properties of controls using XML syntax, which separates UI design from application logic.

- **Advantages:**

- **Readability and Maintainability:** XAML provides a clear, human-readable structure that makes it easier to design, maintain, and modify interfaces.

- **Separation of Concerns:** Designers can work on XAML files while developers focus on the underlying logic in C# or Q#.

- **Reusability:** Styles, templates, and resources can be defined once in XAML and reused throughout the application.

**Example:**

```
<ContentPage xmlns="http://schemas.microsoft.com/dotnet/2021/maui"
        xmlns:x="http://schemas.microsoft.com/winfx/2009/xaml"
        x:Class="QuantumApp.Views.MainPage">
  <ContentPage.Resources>
    <Style x:Key="QuantumLabelStyle" TargetType="Label">
      <Setter Property="TextColor" Value="DarkBlue" />
      <Setter Property="FontSize" Value="Medium" />
    </Style>
  </ContentPage.Resources>
  <StackLayout Padding="20">
    <Label Text="Quantum Circuit Simulator"
        Style="{StaticResource QuantumLabelStyle}"
        HorizontalOptions="Center" />
    <!-- Additional controls will be added here -->
  </StackLayout>
</ContentPage>
```

- 

Layouts

- **Purpose of Layouts:**
  Layouts in .NET MAUI are containers that organize UI elements. They

determine how controls are arranged on the screen and adapt to different device sizes and orientations.

- **Common Layouts:**

  - **StackLayout:**
    Arranges children in a single line, vertically or horizontally. Ideal for simple lists or forms.

  - **Grid:**
    Provides a flexible two-dimensional table-like layout. Suitable for complex interfaces where precise control over rows and columns is needed.

  - **FlexLayout:**
    Offers a flexible box layout model similar to CSS Flexbox, allowing for dynamic arrangement and alignment of children.

  - **AbsoluteLayout and RelativeLayout:**
    Allow positioning of elements using explicit coordinates or relative to other elements.

- **Best Practices:**

  - Use responsive layouts to ensure that your quantum simulator's UI scales elegantly across different platforms.

  - Combine layouts as needed to achieve the desired design; for instance, a Grid might hold multiple StackLayouts to create a multi-pane interface.

Controls

- **Built-In Controls:**

  .NET MAUI includes a variety of controls such as:

  - **Button, Label, Entry, and Picker:** Fundamental building blocks for user interaction.

  - **CollectionView and ListView:** For displaying lists of items—useful for showing simulation parameters or historical results.

  - **GraphicsView:** A powerful control for rendering custom graphics, which is ideal for visualizing quantum states (like Bloch spheres) and circuit diagrams.

- **Custom Controls:**

  Developers can create custom controls to encapsulate complex quantum visualization logic. This ensures consistency across the app and simplifies future modifications.

- **Styling and Theming:**

  Utilize resource dictionaries in XAML to define global styles and themes. This makes it easier to maintain a consistent look and feel across different platforms.

## Implementing the MVVM Design Pattern for Clean Architecture

What is MVVM?

MVVM (Model-View-ViewModel) is a design pattern that separates the user interface (View) from the business logic (Model) through an intermediate layer (ViewModel). This separation facilitates modularity, testability, and maintainability.

Components of MVVM:

- **Model:**
  Represents the core data and business logic. In a quantum simulator app, the model might include classes that represent quantum circuits, simulation parameters, and computational results.

- **View:**
  The visual interface defined in XAML. It contains controls and layouts that display the quantum simulation and interact with the user.

- **ViewModel:**
  Acts as a bridge between the View and the Model. It exposes properties and commands that the View can data-bind to, handling user interactions and updating the Model accordingly.

Benefits for Quantum Applications:

- **Separation of Concerns:**
  By isolating UI from simulation logic, changes in the quantum simulation

code do not impact the user interface, and vice versa.

- **Testability:**
  With logic encapsulated in the ViewModel, unit testing becomes more straightforward. You can test quantum algorithm implementations and state transitions without relying on the UI.

- **Maintainability:**
  Clean separation facilitates easier updates and scalability. For example, adding a new quantum gate or simulation feature can be managed within the Model and ViewModel without major changes to the UI.

Implementing MVVM in .NET MAUI:

**Data Binding:**

XAML's binding syntax allows the View to automatically update when properties in the ViewModel change. For example:

```
<Label Text="{Binding QuantumCircuitName}" />
```

- 

**Commands:**

Commands are used to handle user interactions. A button might bind to a command that initiates a quantum simulation:

```
<Button Text="Simulate Circuit" Command="{Binding
RunSimulationCommand}" />
```

- 

**Example ViewModel:**

```
public class QuantumCircuitViewModel : INotifyPropertyChanged
{
    private string quantumCircuitName;
```

```csharp
public string QuantumCircuitName
{
    get => quantumCircuitName;
    set
    {
        quantumCircuitName = value;
        OnPropertyChanged(nameof(QuantumCircuitName));
    }
}

public ICommand RunSimulationCommand { get; }

public QuantumCircuitViewModel()
{
    QuantumCircuitName = "Default Circuit";
    RunSimulationCommand = new Command(ExecuteRunSimulation);
}

private void ExecuteRunSimulation()
{
    // Logic to run the quantum circuit simulation
    // This could involve calling a service that interacts with Qiskit or Q#
}

public event PropertyChangedEventHandler PropertyChanged;
protected void OnPropertyChanged(string propertyName)
{
    PropertyChanged?.Invoke(this, new
PropertyChangedEventArgs(propertyName));
}
}
```

-

# Data Binding and Navigation in Multi-Platform Apps

Data Binding in .NET MAUI

Data binding is the process of linking UI elements in the View to data sources in the ViewModel, ensuring that the UI reflects the current state of the data.

- **One-Way Binding:**
  Data flows from the ViewModel to the View. Use this for display elements where user input is not expected.

- **Two-Way Binding:**
  Data flows in both directions. This is useful for input controls where changes in the UI update the ViewModel and vice versa (e.g., Entry controls).

- **Binding Modes and Converters:**
  .NET MAUI supports various binding modes (OneTime, OneWay, TwoWay) and allows the use of converters to transform data as it passes between the ViewModel and View.

**Example:**

```
<Entry Text="{Binding QuantumCircuitName, Mode=TwoWay}"
Placeholder="Enter circuit name" />
```

-

Navigation in .NET MAUI

Efficient navigation is essential for building a multi-page quantum simulator app, enabling users to move between different functionalities like circuit building, simulation results, and settings.

- **Navigation Patterns:**

  .NET MAUI supports various navigation paradigms:

  - **Stack Navigation:**

    Pages are pushed and popped off a navigation stack, similar to the way web pages work.

  - **Tabbed Navigation:**

    Provides a tabbed interface for switching between multiple pages or views.

  - **Shell Navigation:**

    Introduced in .NET MAUI, Shell provides a simplified way to organize and navigate multi-page applications. It offers built-in support for flyout menus, tabs, and URL-based navigation.

**Implementing Navigation:**

Using Shell, you can define routes and navigation paths in your application's XAML:

```xml
<Shell xmlns="http://schemas.microsoft.com/dotnet/2021/maui"
    xmlns:x="http://schemas.microsoft.com/winfx/2009/xaml"
    x:Class="QuantumApp.AppShell">
  <TabBar>
    <ShellContent Title="Home" ContentTemplate="{DataTemplate local:HomePage}" />
    <ShellContent Title="Simulator" ContentTemplate="{DataTemplate local:SimulatorPage}" />
    <ShellContent Title="Settings" ContentTemplate="{DataTemplate local:SettingsPage}" />
  </TabBar>
</Shell>
```

-

**Programmatic Navigation:**

Navigation can also be controlled programmatically via commands or methods in the ViewModel:

```
await Shell.Current.GoToAsync("SimulatorPage");
```

- 

- **Navigation Best Practices:**

  - **Consistent UX:** Ensure that the navigation scheme is intuitive and consistent across different platforms.

  - **State Preservation:** Maintain state during navigation, particularly in quantum simulation scenarios where circuit data might be modified.

  - **Deep Linking:** Enable deep linking to allow users to navigate directly to specific screens, which is useful for sharing simulation results or circuit configurations.

The fundamentals of .NET MAUI provide a powerful toolkit for building advanced cross-platform applications, and when applied to quantum simulation, they unlock new possibilities for interactive, high-performance applications. By leveraging XAML for clear and maintainable UI definitions, employing layouts and controls to create responsive designs, and adopting the MVVM design pattern, developers can achieve a clean, modular architecture that separates concerns effectively.

Data binding and sophisticated navigation paradigms further ensure that your application remains robust and user-friendly across various platforms. Whether you are building a quantum circuit editor, a state visualizer, or a comprehensive simulator, the integration of these .NET MAUI fundamentals lays the groundwork for a scalable and engaging quantum application.

In the next sections, we will apply these principles to build specific components of our quantum simulator app, starting with a detailed design of the Quantum Circuit

Builder interface and integrating simulation logic that connects to both local and cloud-based quantum computation services.

# Integrating Quantum Computing Libraries with .NET MAUI

Modern quantum computing is increasingly becoming accessible through robust APIs and software libraries that simulate quantum circuits or even provide access to actual quantum hardware via the cloud. Integrating these quantum computing libraries with a cross-platform framework like .NET MAUI enables developers to build interactive applications that bridge advanced quantum computations with user-friendly interfaces. In this section, we will explore three key topics:

1. **Connecting to Quantum Simulators and APIs**

2. **Building Interactive Visualizations of Quantum Circuits**

3. **Handling Quantum Data and Displaying Algorithm Outcomes**

## Connecting to Quantum Simulators and APIs

Overview

To build a quantum-enabled application, you need to connect your .NET MAUI app with quantum simulators or APIs that process quantum circuits. This connection can be established either via local simulation libraries or through cloud-based quantum services.

Local Quantum Simulators

Many quantum libraries such as Qiskit (Python), Cirq (Python), or even Microsoft's Q# have robust simulation capabilities. You can integrate these with .NET MAUI in a couple of ways:

- **Interoperability with Python Libraries:**
  Using tools like **Python.NET** or by creating a REST API wrapper around a Python-based quantum simulator, you can call functions written in Python from your .NET MAUI application.
  For example, you might create a microservice using Flask that runs Qiskit simulations, and then call this service from your MAUI app using HTTP requests.

- **Direct Integration with Q#:**
  Microsoft's Q# is integrated within the .NET ecosystem. You can call Q# operations from C# code in your MAUI project. This approach enables a seamless development experience using a single language stack and Visual Studio tooling.

Cloud-Based Quantum Services

Several cloud providers now offer quantum computing platforms, allowing you to run experiments on actual quantum hardware:

- **IBM Quantum Experience:**
  Provides an API that allows you to submit quantum circuits written in Qiskit. You can integrate it by invoking the REST API directly from your MAUI app.

- **Microsoft Azure Quantum:**
  Offers access to quantum hardware via Q#. By using Azure SDKs in your MAUI app, you can queue quantum jobs and retrieve results.

- **Amazon Braket:**
  Amazon's service provides both quantum simulators and real quantum processing units (QPUs). Integration is possible through Amazon's SDK for .NET, which facilitates submitting jobs and managing results.

Example Workflow

1. **Circuit Submission:**
   The app captures a quantum circuit design from the user and converts it into the appropriate format (e.g., QASM for Qiskit, or a Q# operation).

2. **API Call:**
   Using HTTP clients or SDK calls in .NET MAUI, the circuit is sent to a cloud-based quantum simulator.

3. **Job Monitoring and Retrieval:**
   The app periodically checks for job completion and then retrieves the results once they are available.

# Building Interactive Visualizations of Quantum Circuits

Visualization Objectives

Interactive visualizations are crucial for understanding and debugging quantum circuits. These visualizations might include:

- **Circuit Diagrams:**
  Graphically represent the sequence of quantum gates acting on each qubit.

- **Bloch Sphere Representations:**
  Visualize the state of single qubits.

- **Probability Distributions:**
  Display measurement outcomes and statistical distributions resulting from quantum computations.

Implementing Visualizations in .NET MAUI

- **GraphicsView Control:**
  .NET MAUI offers a **GraphicsView** control that can be used to render custom drawings. You can create custom renderers to draw circuit diagrams dynamically.

- **Charting Libraries:**
  Use charting libraries that support .NET MAUI (such as Syncfusion, Telerik, or open-source alternatives) to plot probability distributions, histograms, or line charts that reflect simulation outcomes.

- **Interactive UI Elements:**
  Incorporate gestures (like pinch-to-zoom and pan) for detailed circuit exploration. Users can tap on a gate to see more details or to modify its parameters.

Example: Drawing a Quantum Circuit

Consider a simple scenario where you want to draw a circuit with qubits and gate icons:

```
<GraphicsView x:Name="CircuitView" HeightRequest="300"
WidthRequest="400" />
```

In the code-behind, you could override the drawing logic:

```
public class CircuitDrawable : IDrawable
{
```

```
public void Draw(ICanvas canvas, RectF dirtyRect)
{
    // Example: Draw two horizontal lines representing qubits
    float spacing = 50;
    canvas.StrokeColor = Colors.Black;
    canvas.DrawLine(0, spacing, dirtyRect.Width, spacing);
    canvas.DrawLine(0, spacing * 2, dirtyRect.Width, spacing * 2);


    // Draw a gate (e.g., a Hadamard gate) on the first qubit
    float gateWidth = 30;
    float gateHeight = 30;
    canvas.FillColor = Colors.LightBlue;
    canvas.FillRectangle(100, spacing - gateHeight / 2, gateWidth, gateHeight);
    canvas.DrawRectangle(100, spacing - gateHeight / 2, gateWidth, gateHeight);


    // Add text to indicate the gate type
    canvas.FontColor = Colors.Black;
    canvas.DrawString("H", 100, spacing - gateHeight / 2,
HorizontalAlignment.Center);
    }
}
```

In your MAUI page, you set the drawable:

CircuitView.Drawable = new CircuitDrawable();

This simple example demonstrates how you can create a dynamic, interactive quantum circuit diagram within your application.

## Handling Quantum Data and Displaying Algorithm Outcomes

Quantum Data Representation

Quantum algorithms produce data that is often probabilistic and complex in nature. Key aspects of quantum data include:

- **Measurement Results:**
  Represented as probabilities for different outcomes, which can be displayed as histograms or pie charts.

- **State Vectors and Density Matrices:**
  These mathematical representations of quantum states may need to be visualized (e.g., using Bloch spheres for single qubits).

- **Error Metrics and Fidelity:**
  Quantitative measures that indicate the performance of quantum algorithms and error-correction processes.

Processing and Displaying Outcomes

- **Data Parsing and Transformation:**
  When quantum results are retrieved from simulators or APIs, they typically arrive in JSON or another structured format. Your application must parse this data, convert it into a suitable format, and compute any additional

metrics such as fidelity or entropy.

- **Visualization of Results:**
  Utilize chart controls to display:

  - **Probability Histograms:** Show the distribution of measurement outcomes.

  - **Line or Bar Charts:** Compare simulation results across multiple runs.

  - **Bloch Sphere Visualizations:** Use custom graphics to represent the quantum state of individual qubits.

- **Interactive Data Exploration:**
  Provide features such as tooltips, zoom, and filters so users can delve deeper into the simulation outcomes. For example, tapping on a histogram bar might display the exact probability or the corresponding circuit configuration that led to that outcome.

Example: Displaying a Histogram of Measurement Outcomes

Suppose you have simulation results that yield the following measurement probabilities for a 3-qubit circuit:

```
var measurementResults = new Dictionary<string, double>

{

    {"000", 0.35},

    {"001", 0.10},

    {"010", 0.15},

    {"011", 0.05},
```

```
    {"100", 0.10},

    {"101", 0.05},

    {"110", 0.15},

    {"111", 0.05}

};
```

You could use a chart control to display this data. For instance, using a hypothetical ChartView in .NET MAUI:

```
<ChartView x:Name="ResultsChart" HeightRequest="300"
WidthRequest="400"/>
```

In your code-behind, bind the data to the chart:

```
public void DisplayMeasurementResults(Dictionary<string, double> results)

{

    var chartEntries = results.Select(result => new ChartEntry((float)result.Value)

    {

        Label = result.Key,

        ValueLabel = $"{result.Value:P1}",

        Color = SkiaSharp.SKColor.Parse("#3498db")

    }).ToList();


    ResultsChart.Chart = new BarChart { Entries = chartEntries };
```

```
}
```

This example converts raw measurement probabilities into a bar chart that users can easily interpret.

Integrating quantum computing libraries with .NET MAUI opens the door to powerful, interactive applications that make quantum computing accessible to a broader audience. By connecting to local simulators or cloud-based quantum services, you can execute quantum algorithms directly from your MAUI app. Meanwhile, interactive visualizations—such as custom circuit diagrams, Bloch sphere renderings, and dynamic charts—provide users with deep insights into how quantum circuits operate and perform.

Handling quantum data effectively involves not only parsing complex, probabilistic output but also transforming it into meaningful visual representations that highlight the strengths and challenges of quantum algorithms. These integrations ultimately create a seamless experience where advanced quantum computations are brought to life through modern, user-friendly application interfaces.

In subsequent sections, we will further develop these components, delving into more advanced features like real-time simulation updates, deeper error analysis, and integrating feedback mechanisms to improve both the simulation accuracy and the overall user experience.

# Advanced .NET MAUI Techniques for Quantum App Development

In this section, we delve into advanced techniques for developing sophisticated quantum applications using .NET MAUI. As quantum apps require real-time data visualization, high performance, and a smooth user experience across platforms, developers must leverage custom controls, optimize performance, and incorporate accessibility and responsive design. Below is an extensive exploration of these topics.

## Custom Controls for Real-Time Quantum State Visualization

Quantum applications often require real-time visual feedback to represent complex phenomena such as qubit states, superposition, and entanglement. Custom controls in .NET MAUI enable you to build tailored visualization components that provide interactive, dynamic displays of quantum information.

Key Objectives:

- **Dynamic Rendering of Quantum States:**
  Visualize qubit states using dynamic graphics—such as Bloch spheres—that update in real time as users interact with quantum circuits or simulation parameters.

- **Circuit Diagram Visualization:**

  Create custom controls to represent quantum circuit diagrams, showing the sequential application of quantum gates on qubits. This control can allow zooming, panning, and detailed inspection of individual gate operations.

- **Interactive Elements:**

  Incorporate user interaction to allow selection, editing, and real-time updates of quantum simulation parameters. For example, tapping on a visual element might bring up details about the gate's action or the quantum state's probability distribution.

Implementing Custom Controls:

**Using GraphicsView:**

.NET MAUI's GraphicsView control is ideal for creating custom drawing logic. By implementing the IDrawable interface, you can render complex visualizations such as:

```
public class BlochSphereDrawable : IDrawable

{

   public QuantumState QubitState { get; set; }  // Custom model representing
qubit state


   public void Draw(ICanvas canvas, RectF dirtyRect)

   {

   // Clear background

   canvas.FillColor = Colors.White;

   canvas.FillRectangle(dirtyRect);
```

```
// Draw a simple circle representing the Bloch sphere

float centerX = dirtyRect.MidX;

float centerY = dirtyRect.MidY;

float radius = Math.Min(dirtyRect.Width, dirtyRect.Height) / 2 - 10;

canvas.StrokeColor = Colors.Black;

canvas.DrawCircle(centerX, centerY, radius);


// Draw a marker indicating the qubit state on the sphere

// Convert the qubit state into spherical coordinates (theta, phi)

float theta = QubitState.Theta;  // Angle from the positive Z-axis

float phi = QubitState.Phi;      // Azimuthal angle in the X-Y plane


// Project the state onto the 2D Bloch sphere view

float markerX = centerX + radius * (float)(Math.Sin(theta) * Math.Cos(phi));

float markerY = centerY - radius * (float)(Math.Sin(theta) * Math.Sin(phi)); // Invert Y-axis for screen coordinates


canvas.FillColor = Colors.Red;

canvas.FillCircle(markerX, markerY, 5);

    }

}
```

●

**Integrating in XAML:**

You can embed your custom drawable control into your MAUI page by creating a GraphicsView and assigning your custom drawable:

```xml
<ContentPage xmlns="http://schemas.microsoft.com/dotnet/2021/maui"

        xmlns:x="http://schemas.microsoft.com/winfx/2009/xaml"

        x:Class="QuantumApp.Views.BlochSpherePage">

  <StackLayout Padding="20">

    <Label Text="Qubit State Visualization"

        HorizontalOptions="Center"

        FontAttributes="Bold" />

    <GraphicsView x:Name="blochSphereView"

        HeightRequest="300"

        WidthRequest="300"/>

  </StackLayout>

</ContentPage>
```

In the code-behind, assign the drawable:

```csharp
public partial class BlochSpherePage : ContentPage

{

  public BlochSpherePage()

  {

    InitializeComponent();
```

```
var drawable = new BlochSphereDrawable

{

    QubitState = new QuantumState { Theta = (float)Math.PI / 4, Phi =
(float)Math.PI / 3 }

};

blochSphereView.Drawable = drawable;

}

}
```

- 

Custom controls such as these are essential for providing intuitive, real-time feedback in quantum applications, making abstract concepts accessible through visual representations.

## Performance Optimization and Cross-Platform Debugging

Quantum simulations and complex UI renderings can be computationally intensive. To ensure a smooth user experience, optimizing performance and effective debugging across platforms are crucial.

Performance Optimization Techniques:

- **Efficient Rendering:**

    - **Minimize Overdraw:** Use layering strategies and only redraw regions that have changed.

    - **Hardware Acceleration:** Leverage GPU-accelerated rendering in .NET MAUI's GraphicsView for smoother animations and complex drawings.

- **Asynchronous Operations:** Offload heavy computations, such as quantum simulation calculations, to background threads using asynchronous programming to avoid blocking the UI thread.

- **Memory Management:**

  - **Optimize Object Lifetimes:** Dispose of unused objects and controls to free up memory.

  - **Use Value Types Where Appropriate:** Avoid unnecessary allocations by using structs or Span for data processing.

- **Profiling and Benchmarking:**

  - Use .NET's built-in performance profiling tools to monitor CPU and memory usage.

  - Integrate cross-platform debugging tools such as Visual Studio's Diagnostic Tools to capture performance metrics on Windows, macOS, and mobile devices.

Cross-Platform Debugging Best Practices:

- **Platform-Specific Testing:**
  Ensure that the app is tested on all targeted platforms. Emulators and physical devices can reveal platform-specific performance bottlenecks or UI issues.

- **Logging and Diagnostics:**
  Implement structured logging using frameworks like Microsoft.Extensions.Logging to capture runtime information. Logs should be platform-aware and include device-specific context to aid in

troubleshooting.

- **Conditional Compilation:**
  Use conditional compilation directives (#if ANDROID, #if IOS, etc.) to implement or debug platform-specific code without affecting the global codebase.

- **Remote Debugging:**
  Take advantage of remote debugging tools provided by Visual Studio or platform-specific debuggers to diagnose issues on devices that are not physically accessible.

By combining these strategies, you can ensure that your quantum simulator application remains performant and responsive, even as it handles complex simulations and real-time visualizations.

## Enhancing User Experience: Accessibility, Responsive Design, and Animations

A great application not only performs well but also provides an engaging and inclusive user experience. For quantum applications, this means designing interfaces that are accessible, responsive, and visually appealing.

Accessibility

- **Inclusive Design Principles:**
  Ensure that the app is usable by people with a range of abilities. This includes:

  - **Screen Readers:** Use semantic XAML elements (e.g., proper labeling of buttons, controls, and images) to ensure compatibility with screen readers.

- **High Contrast Modes:** Offer themes that support high contrast for users with visual impairments.

- **Text Scaling:** Ensure that text elements are dynamic and support system-wide font scaling.

- **Implementation Techniques:**

Use the AutomationProperties class in XAML to provide descriptive labels for UI elements:

<Button Text="Run Simulation"

    AutomationProperties.Name="Run Quantum Simulation"

    AutomationProperties.HelpText="Starts the simulation of the quantum circuit" />

    o

Responsive Design

- **Adaptive Layouts:**
  With .NET MAUI, design UIs that adapt to different screen sizes and orientations. Use layouts such as **Grid** and **FlexLayout** to create fluid interfaces that adjust automatically.

- **Scalable Graphics:**
  Use vector-based graphics and scalable UI elements to ensure that visualizations (e.g., quantum circuit diagrams and Bloch spheres) remain sharp and clear on devices of all sizes.

- **Testing on Multiple Devices:**
  Utilize emulators and device simulators to test the app's responsiveness. Pay attention to both portrait and landscape modes, ensuring that critical

functionalities remain accessible regardless of screen orientation.

Animations

- **Purpose of Animations:**
  Animations can improve user engagement by providing visual cues during state changes. For a quantum simulator, animations can be used to:

  - Highlight transitions in quantum states.

  - Smoothly reveal simulation results.

  - Provide feedback when users interact with custom controls.

**Implementing Animations in .NET MAUI:**
.NET MAUI supports built-in animation APIs. For example, to animate the transition of a control's opacity:

```
await myControl.FadeTo(0.5, 500);  // Fade control to 50% opacity over 500ms

await myControl.FadeTo(1, 500);    // Fade back to full opacity over 500ms
```

- 
- **Advanced Animation Techniques:**

  - **Storyboard-like Sequences:** Create complex sequences by chaining animations together.

  - **Interactive Animations:** Enable animations that respond to user gestures, such as swiping or tapping, to provide a more immersive experience.

  - **Optimized Animation Performance:** Ensure that animations run smoothly on all devices by minimizing unnecessary redraws and using hardware acceleration where possible.

Advanced .NET MAUI techniques can dramatically enhance the functionality, performance, and user experience of quantum applications. By building custom controls for real-time quantum state visualization, you transform abstract quantum data into interactive, intuitive graphics. Performance optimization and effective cross-platform debugging ensure that your app remains responsive and efficient, even under the demands of complex simulations.

Finally, focusing on accessibility, responsive design, and engaging animations not only improves the aesthetic appeal of your quantum simulator but also ensures that it is inclusive and user-friendly across diverse devices and user needs. These advanced techniques empower developers to bridge the gap between cutting-edge quantum computing research and practical, high-quality software solutions.

In the next section, we will consolidate these concepts with a detailed case study that walks through the complete development of a quantum simulator application, integrating all the advanced .NET MAUI techniques discussed here.

# Practical Projects

This section examines real-world applications of quantum computing integrated with modern cross-platform development using .NET MAUI. We will explore an end-to-end walkthrough of developing a quantum circuit simulator mobile app, discuss deployment strategies for iOS, Android, Windows, and macOS, and review lessons learned and best practices gleaned from real-world projects.

## End-to-End Walkthrough: Developing a Quantum Circuit Simulator Mobile App

Project Overview

The quantum circuit simulator mobile app is designed to allow users to create, simulate, and visualize quantum circuits interactively. Users can build circuits by dragging and dropping quantum gates, execute the circuit on a simulated quantum backend, and view the output as graphical representations (e.g., circuit diagrams, Bloch spheres, or probability histograms).

Key Functionalities

- **Circuit Editor:**
  A visual interface for constructing quantum circuits. Users can select qubits, drag quantum gates (Hadamard, CNOT, Pauli-X, etc.), and position them on a timeline.

- **Simulation Engine:**
  Integration with quantum simulation libraries (e.g., Microsoft Q#, Qiskit, or Cirq) that execute the designed circuits either locally or via cloud APIs.

- **Visualization Components:**
  Real-time visual feedback including custom controls for quantum state visualization (e.g., a dynamic Bloch sphere) and circuit diagrams.

- **Results Display:**
  Statistical displays of measurement outcomes, error rates, and simulation metrics.

Development Phases

1. **Requirement Analysis & Planning:**

   - **Define Scope:** Establish core features (circuit building, simulation, visualization).

   - **Choose Tools:** Utilize .NET MAUI for UI, Q# for simulation integration, and appropriate third-party libraries for visualization (e.g., SkiaSharp).

   - **Architecture:** Adopt the MVVM pattern to separate business logic (quantum simulation, data processing) from the UI.

2. **Design & Prototyping:**

   - **UI/UX Design:** Create wireframes for the circuit editor, simulation dashboard, and results view.

   - **Data Model:** Define models for quantum circuits, gates, and qubit states.

   - **Prototype Custom Controls:** Build early prototypes of the GraphicsView-based Bloch sphere and circuit diagram components.

3. **Implementation:**

**Circuit Editor:**
Develop a drag-and-drop interface using XAML and MAUI layouts (e.g., Grid and StackLayout). Use custom controls to represent gates and qubits.

Example snippet (XAML for a gate palette):

```xml
<StackLayout Orientation="Horizontal" Padding="10">
  <Button Text="H" Command="{Binding AddHadamardCommand}" />
  <Button Text="X" Command="{Binding AddPauliXCommand}" />
  <Button Text="CNOT" Command="{Binding AddCNOTCommand}" />
</StackLayout>
```

  o

**Simulation Integration:**
Implement services that convert the visual circuit into a quantum circuit representation. For Q# integration, use the Quantum Development Kit libraries to compile and run circuits:

```
var result = await
QuantumSimulatorService.RunCircuitAsync(quantumCircuitData);
```

  o

  o **Visualization:**
    Use custom renderers and GraphicsView controls to dynamically display quantum circuits and state visualizations. The Bloch sphere, for instance, should update in real time as simulation parameters change.

  o **Data Binding & Navigation:**
    Apply MVVM for clean separation. Use data binding to synchronize simulation outcomes with visual components, and employ Shell navigation for multi-page transitions.

4. **Testing & Debugging:**

○ **Unit Tests:** Write tests for circuit conversion, simulation service, and custom controls.

○ **Cross-Platform Testing:** Ensure that the app's UI and simulation functionalities work seamlessly on iOS, Android, Windows, and macOS emulators or devices.

○ **Performance Profiling:** Use Visual Studio diagnostic tools to optimize rendering and background computations.

5. **Deployment:**

○ Package and deploy the app using platform-specific tools (discussed in detail below).

# Deployment Strategies for iOS, Android, Windows, and macOS

Deploying a cross-platform quantum simulator app built with .NET MAUI requires tailored strategies for each target platform while leveraging MAUI's single-codebase advantages.

iOS

● **Development Environment:**

○ Use a Mac with Xcode installed for iOS development.

○ Visual Studio 2022 for Mac or Visual Studio with paired Mac build host.

- **Deployment Steps:**

  - Build and test using the iOS Simulator.

  - Configure provisioning profiles, certificates, and entitlements for App Store submission.

  - Use Apple's TestFlight for beta testing and feedback.

- **Considerations:**

  - Ensure that the UI is optimized for various iOS screen sizes.

  - Leverage iOS-specific APIs (if needed) through dependency services.

Android

- **Development Environment:**

  - Android SDK and emulator setup integrated with Visual Studio.

  - Testing on multiple devices/emulators to cover a range of screen sizes and Android versions.

- **Deployment Steps:**

  - Optimize performance for various Android hardware configurations.

  - Configure AndroidManifest.xml with proper permissions.

  - Sign the APK and deploy via Google Play Console.

- **Considerations:**

  - Handle device fragmentation; test on multiple devices.

  - Optimize for battery consumption and resource usage.

Windows

- **Development Environment:**

  - Utilize Visual Studio on Windows with the latest Windows SDK.

- **Deployment Steps:**

  - Test on both desktop and tablet devices to ensure responsive design.

  - Configure UWP or WinUI settings as per application requirements.

  - Package the application using MSIX and distribute through the Microsoft Store or enterprise deployment.

- **Considerations:**

  - Leverage Windows-specific integrations such as notifications and live tiles.

  - Ensure keyboard and mouse interactions are well-supported.

macOS

- **Development Environment:**

  - Visual Studio for Mac or Visual Studio Code with MAUI support.

- **Deployment Steps:**

  - Test using macOS's built-in simulation environment.

  - Configure signing and notarization required by Apple.

  - Distribute through the Mac App Store or via direct downloads.

- **Considerations:**

  - Ensure that the app complies with macOS UI guidelines.

  - Optimize for retina displays and various macOS window sizes.

Cross-Platform Deployment Best Practices

- **Automated Build Pipelines:**
  Implement CI/CD pipelines using GitHub Actions, Azure DevOps, or similar services that support multi-target builds. Automate testing, signing, and deployment processes to streamline releases.

- **Configuration Management:**
  Use MAUI's platform-specific resources to adjust settings, assets, and configurations for each target platform without duplicating code.

- **Testing and Beta Programs:**
  Leverage beta testing platforms (TestFlight for iOS, Google Play's beta track, Windows Insider) to gather feedback and identify platform-specific issues before public release.

## Lessons Learned and Best Practices from Real-World Projects

Drawing from various case studies and practical projects, several key lessons and best practices emerge for developing and deploying quantum applications using .NET MAUI.

Key Lessons Learned:

- **Iterative Development is Critical:**
  Developing complex apps like a quantum simulator benefits greatly from iterative design, where early prototypes are tested and refined based on user feedback.

- **Modularity Enhances Flexibility:**
  Using patterns such as MVVM allows for a clean separation between the simulation logic and the user interface. This modularity makes the app easier to maintain and extend, as components can be updated independently.

- **Performance Optimization Must be Integrated Early:**
  Advanced simulations and real-time visualizations can be resource-intensive. Profiling and optimizing performance early in the development cycle helps prevent bottlenecks later on.

- **Cross-Platform Consistency Requires Rigorous Testing:**
  Even with a shared codebase, differences in platform behavior can arise. Testing on multiple devices and using automated tools helps ensure a consistent user experience across platforms.

- **User Experience is Paramount:**
  Features like accessibility, responsive design, and smooth animations are not merely cosmetic; they are essential for ensuring that complex quantum information is conveyed effectively to users.

Best Practices:

- **Embrace the Power of MVVM:**
  Adopt the MVVM pattern from the outset. It provides a robust structure that separates concerns, enhances testability, and simplifies UI updates as simulation logic evolves.

- **Utilize Custom Controls Wisely:**
  Invest time in building custom controls for specialized tasks such as quantum circuit visualization and Bloch sphere rendering. These controls add significant value by turning abstract quantum data into intuitive visual representations.

- **Optimize for the User:**
  Prioritize accessibility features, including screen reader support, dynamic font scaling, and high contrast themes. A quantum simulator app should be usable by a diverse audience, including those new to quantum computing.

- **Integrate with Cloud Services Early:**
  Design your app with future cloud integration in mind. Whether using IBM Quantum Experience, Azure Quantum, or another provider, creating a flexible API integration layer allows you to switch between simulators and real hardware with minimal code changes.

- **Automate Testing and Deployment:**
  Implement a CI/CD pipeline that covers automated builds, tests, and deployment for all target platforms. This practice minimizes manual intervention, reduces errors, and speeds up the release cycle.

- **Document Thoroughly:**
  Maintain comprehensive documentation for your code, architecture, and design decisions. This is especially important in interdisciplinary projects that bridge quantum computing and mobile app development.

Building a quantum simulator application using .NET MAUI is an ambitious yet highly rewarding endeavor. Through an end-to-end development process, we can create a robust, interactive platform that brings quantum circuit simulation to users across iOS, Android, Windows, and macOS. By following strategic deployment practices and learning from real-world projects, developers can overcome common challenges and deliver a seamless, engaging experience.

The lessons learned—from embracing modular architectures and optimizing performance to ensuring cross-platform consistency and accessibility—provide invaluable guidance for future quantum app development projects. As quantum computing continues to mature, these practical experiences will serve as the foundation for more sophisticated applications that not only simulate but eventually harness quantum computations to solve real-world problems.

In the subsequent chapters, we will explore emerging trends and additional features that further integrate quantum algorithms into cross-platform applications, paving the way for the next generation of quantum-enhanced software solutions.

# Future Trends and Emerging Research

Quantum computing is an evolving frontier with rapid progress in both hardware and algorithmic techniques. As research pushes the boundaries of what's possible, emerging trends point toward a convergence between quantum computing, artificial intelligence, and modern cross-platform development. This section provides an extensive overview of anticipated advances, the interplay between these fields, and an outlook on quantum computing applications across industry sectors.

## Advances in Quantum Hardware and Algorithms

Quantum Hardware Innovations

- **Scalability and Qubit Quality:**
  Significant research is focused on increasing the number of qubits while maintaining or improving their coherence times and gate fidelities. Advances in superconducting qubits, trapped ions, and silicon-based qubits are pushing hardware toward error rates below the threshold needed for fault-tolerant computation.

  - **Superconducting Circuits:**
    Research continues to refine fabrication processes and error correction in superconducting systems, with many companies reporting improvements in qubit connectivity and coherence.

  - **Trapped Ion Systems:**
    Trapped ion qubits benefit from long coherence times and high-fidelity gate operations. Emerging techniques in ion shuttling and scalable trap architectures are expected to further enhance their

capabilities.

- ○ **Topological Qubits:**
  Although still in an experimental stage, topological qubits, which store information in the global properties of a system, promise inherent error resistance by their very nature. These systems could potentially revolutionize fault tolerance in quantum computing.

- **Hybrid Quantum-Classical Architectures:**
  As fully error-corrected quantum computers remain a future goal, hybrid architectures that combine classical processors with NISQ (Noisy Intermediate-Scale Quantum) devices are emerging. These systems allow quantum processors to accelerate specific tasks while classical systems manage overall operations and error mitigation strategies.

Algorithmic Breakthroughs

- **New Quantum Algorithms:**
  Beyond the well-known algorithms like Shor's for factoring and Grover's for search, research is expanding into algorithms tailored for:

  - ○ **Optimization:**
    Variational Quantum Eigensolvers (VQE) and the Quantum Approximate Optimization Algorithm (QAOA) are among the leading candidates for solving optimization problems in chemistry, logistics, and finance.

  - ○ **Machine Learning:**
    Quantum algorithms for machine learning are exploring applications in data classification, clustering, and pattern recognition. Quantum-enhanced algorithms promise speedups for processing large, complex datasets.

- ○ **Simulation of Quantum Systems:**
  Quantum simulation remains one of the most promising applications. Advances in simulation algorithms could allow for modeling complex molecular systems and materials with unprecedented precision.

- **Error Correction and Noise Resilience:**
  Ongoing research into quantum error correction continues to refine codes and fault-tolerant architectures. Techniques such as surface codes and concatenated coding are expected to improve the reliability of quantum operations, which is critical for scaling up quantum computations.

- **Algorithm Optimization:**
  With improvements in both hardware and simulation techniques, quantum algorithms will be further optimized for specific hardware architectures. This co-design process, where algorithms are tailored to the strengths and limitations of available quantum hardware, will be a major area of innovation.

# The Convergence of Quantum Computing, AI, and Cross-Platform Development

Quantum and Artificial Intelligence Integration

- **Quantum Machine Learning (QML):**
  The intersection of quantum computing and AI is spawning a new discipline known as quantum machine learning. QML seeks to leverage quantum algorithms to solve machine learning tasks more efficiently than classical algorithms. For instance:

  - ○ **Speeding Up Linear Algebra Operations:**
    Many machine learning algorithms rely on matrix operations, and quantum algorithms have the potential to accelerate these

computations significantly.

- ○ **Quantum Neural Networks:**
  Researchers are exploring how quantum circuits can mimic neural network architectures, potentially leading to models that learn faster or capture more complex patterns.

- **Data-Driven Quantum Control:**
  AI techniques are being employed to optimize quantum control parameters, improving the stability and performance of quantum hardware. Machine learning models can predict optimal pulse sequences and error mitigation strategies to enhance qubit coherence and gate fidelity.

Cross-Platform Development and Quantum Applications

- **Unified Application Frameworks:**
  The use of frameworks like .NET MAUI enables the development of applications that can integrate quantum computing capabilities into user-friendly interfaces across multiple platforms (iOS, Android, Windows, macOS). This convergence allows quantum insights to be delivered as interactive apps for research, education, and commercial use.

- **Hybrid Cloud Architectures:**
  Quantum computing services are increasingly accessible through cloud-based APIs (IBM Quantum, Azure Quantum, Amazon Braket). Cross-platform applications can integrate these services, providing a seamless user experience where complex quantum computations are performed remotely while results are visualized locally.

- **Interdisciplinary Collaboration Tools:**
  As quantum computing begins to intersect with fields like AI and mobile development, cross-platform apps become a natural medium for collaboration between scientists, engineers, and developers. Such tools facilitate real-time data visualization, remote simulation, and interactive

debugging of quantum algorithms.

# Outlook for Quantum Computing Applications in Industry

Sector-Specific Applications

- **Pharmaceuticals and Chemistry:**
  Quantum simulations can model molecular interactions at an unprecedented level of detail, accelerating drug discovery and material science research. Companies are already investing in quantum chemistry to predict the behavior of complex biological molecules and novel compounds.

- **Financial Services:**
  Financial institutions are exploring quantum algorithms for portfolio optimization, risk analysis, and fraud detection. The ability of quantum computers to solve complex optimization problems could lead to more accurate models and faster decision-making.

- **Logistics and Supply Chain Management:**
  Quantum algorithms have the potential to optimize routing, scheduling, and resource allocation in logistics. These improvements could lead to significant cost savings and efficiency gains in supply chain operations.

- **Cybersecurity:**
  While quantum computing poses a threat to classical cryptography, it also offers tools for developing unbreakable encryption methods through quantum key distribution (QKD). The advent of quantum-resistant cryptography is a priority for governments and industries to safeguard sensitive data.

- **Artificial Intelligence and Big Data:**
  Quantum-enhanced machine learning algorithms promise to process and analyze massive datasets more efficiently than classical counterparts. This

could revolutionize areas such as pattern recognition, natural language processing, and predictive analytics.

Challenges and Considerations

- **Integration with Legacy Systems:**
  Many industries rely on legacy systems that may not be quantum-ready. Transitioning to quantum-enhanced solutions will require careful integration strategies and transitional architectures.

- **Skill Gap and Workforce Training:**
  The rapid evolution of quantum technologies necessitates new skills. Industries will need to invest in training and development programs to build a workforce capable of harnessing quantum computing.

- **Investment and Infrastructure:**
  Quantum hardware is still expensive and resource-intensive. As technology matures, economies of scale and improved manufacturing techniques are expected to lower costs and broaden accessibility.

- **Regulatory and Ethical Implications:**
  The disruptive potential of quantum computing raises important regulatory and ethical questions, particularly in areas like data privacy and national security. Collaborative efforts among governments, industry, and academia will be essential to develop robust guidelines and standards.

Future Impact

Over the next decade, quantum computing is expected to transition from experimental demonstrations to practical applications. As hardware reliability improves and algorithms become more refined, quantum computing will likely become an integral part of various industrial processes. Early adopters in research-intensive sectors will pave the way for broader commercial applications, transforming industries through enhanced computational power and innovative solutions.

The future of quantum computing is marked by rapid advancements in both hardware and algorithm development, and its convergence with AI and cross-platform application frameworks is opening new frontiers for innovation. By integrating quantum computing capabilities into modern application ecosystems, industries can leverage unparalleled computational power to solve complex problems, optimize operations, and drive new business models.

As research continues to overcome current challenges—such as noise, error correction, and hardware scalability—the impact of quantum computing will extend across sectors, from pharmaceuticals and finance to logistics and cybersecurity. In this dynamic landscape, the collaborative integration of quantum computing, AI, and cross-platform development not only enhances technical capabilities but also creates new opportunities for transformative industrial applications.

In the coming years, as quantum technologies mature and become more accessible, we can expect to see a growing number of applications that harness the power of quantum mechanics, fundamentally reshaping how industries approach computation and problem-solving.

# Appendices

The appendices provide supplementary material to enhance your understanding and streamline your development process. They serve as a quick reference for the essential mathematical tools, a guide to .NET MAUI development resources, and a comprehensive glossary of terms that bridge the domains of quantum computing and cross-platform app development. Below is an extensive overview of each appendix.

## Appendix A: Mathematical Tools and Notations for Quantum Computing

Quantum computing is built on a foundation of sophisticated mathematics. This appendix gathers key mathematical concepts, tools, and notations that are indispensable for understanding and developing quantum algorithms.

Core Mathematical Concepts

- **Linear Algebra:**

  - **Vector Spaces and Hilbert Spaces:**
    Quantum states are represented as vectors in a complex Hilbert space. Familiarity with basis vectors, subspaces, and the concept of orthonormality is essential.

  - **Inner Products and Norms:**
    The inner product defines the "overlap" between quantum states and is used to compute probabilities. For state vectors $|\psi\rangle$ \psi\rangle and $|\phi\rangle$ \phi\rangle, the inner product $\langle \phi | \psi \rangle$ \langle \phi | \psi \rangle is

central to understanding measurement outcomes.

- ○ **Matrices and Operators:**
  Operators acting on quantum states—such as quantum gates—are represented as matrices. Special classes include unitary operators (which preserve norms) and Hermitian operators (representing observables with real eigenvalues).

- ○ **Eigenvalues and Eigenvectors:**
  Many quantum operations require diagonalizing operators. Eigenvalues correspond to measurement outcomes, and eigenvectors define the states associated with these outcomes.

- **Tensor Products:**

  - ○ **Composite Systems:**
    The state space of a multi-qubit system is the tensor product of individual qubit spaces. Understanding tensor products is crucial for grasping concepts like entanglement.

  - ○ **Notation and Properties:**
    Learn to manipulate expressions involving tensor products, which often appear in the representation of composite quantum states and operations.

- **Probability Theory and Statistics:**

  - ○ **Probability Amplitudes:**
    In quantum mechanics, probabilities are derived from the squared magnitudes of complex probability amplitudes.

  - ○ **Normalization and Statistical Interpretation:**
    Quantum states must be normalized, and repeated measurements yield statistical distributions that are analyzed using classical

probability theory.

- ○ **Entropy Measures:**
  Concepts such as von Neumann entropy, mutual information, and conditional entropy quantify uncertainty and information content in quantum systems.

- ● **Complex Numbers and Phases:**

  - ○ **Complex Arithmetic:**
    Since quantum states and operators are defined over complex numbers, proficiency in complex arithmetic, including polar representation and Euler's formula, is vital.

  - ○ **Phase and Interference:**
    The relative phase between components of a superposition leads to interference effects, which are exploited in many quantum algorithms.

Notations and Conventions

- ● **Dirac Notation:**

  - ○ **Kets and Bras:**
    States are denoted as $|\psi\rangle$\psi\rangle (kets) and their dual vectors as $\langle\psi|$\langle\psi| (bras). This notation succinctly represents inner products and outer products.

  - ○ **Projection Operators:**
    Operators like $|\psi\rangle\langle\psi|$\psi\rangle\langle\psi| are used to project states onto a specific vector, an important concept in measurement theory.

- **Matrix Representations:**

  - **Pauli Matrices:**
    The Pauli matrices XX, YY, and ZZ are used to represent basic quantum operations and are essential in describing qubit dynamics.

  - **Unitary and Hermitian Operators:**
    Understand the properties and implications of these operators in terms of reversibility and observability.

This appendix serves as a compact yet thorough reference to the mathematical language of quantum computing, enabling you to better understand the theory behind the algorithms and simulations discussed throughout the book.

## Appendix B: .NET MAUI Development Resources and Sample Code

This appendix is dedicated to providing a collection of development resources, sample code, and tools to help you get started and excel in .NET MAUI app development—particularly for quantum simulation applications.

Key Resources

- **Official Documentation:**

  - **.NET MAUI Documentation:**
    Access the official .NET MAUI documentation for guides, tutorials, and API references.

  - **Quantum SDKs and Tools:**

- **Microsoft Quantum Development Kit (QDK) and Q#:**
  Explore the QDK documentation for tutorials and examples.

- **IBM Quantum Experience and Qiskit:**
  Visit the IBM Quantum Experience and Qiskit documentation for resources and sample notebooks.

- **Google Cirq:**
  Check out Cirq's GitHub repository and official documentation for examples and tutorials.

- **Community Forums and Blogs:**

  - **.NET MAUI Community Toolkit:**
    Learn from the open-source MAUI Community Toolkit which includes reusable controls, converters, and helpers.

  - **Quantum Computing Blogs:**
    Subscribe to blogs like Quantum Country, IBM Research Blog, and Microsoft Quantum Blog for the latest updates and tutorials.

Sample Code Repositories

- **Quantum Simulator App Samples:**

  - **GitHub Repositories:**
    Look for sample projects on GitHub such as:

    - **Quantum Circuit Simulator for .NET MAUI:** A sample project that integrates Q# simulation with a custom-built circuit editor.

- **Cross-Platform Quantum Visualizer:** Projects that provide interactive Bloch sphere and circuit diagram visualizations.

  ○ **Code Snippets:**
    The repository should include examples for:

    - Custom controls for drawing quantum circuits using GraphicsView.

    - Data binding and MVVM implementation for simulation parameters.

    - Integration code for calling quantum simulation APIs (e.g., from Qiskit or Azure Quantum).

- **Templates and Boilerplate:**
  Consider using or adapting templates that provide a pre-configured .NET MAUI project structure. Many open-source projects or sample applications provide a good starting point for building quantum-enabled apps.

Development Tools and Plugins

- **Visual Studio Extensions:**
  Extensions for .NET MAUI and Q# can streamline development. The Q# extension, for example, provides syntax highlighting, IntelliSense, and debugging support within Visual Studio.

- **Cross-Platform Emulators and Device Simulators:**
  Utilize Android emulators, iOS simulators, and desktop testing environments to ensure that your application performs well across all target platforms.

This appendix is your go-to reference for practical tools and sample code that will accelerate your development process. Whether you are new to .NET MAUI or quantum programming, these resources are curated to help you build, test, and deploy high-quality applications.

# Appendix C: Glossary of Quantum and .NET MAUI Terms

A well-defined glossary is crucial for ensuring clarity when navigating the diverse terminologies of quantum computing and cross-platform app development. This appendix provides definitions and explanations for key terms and concepts used throughout the book.

Quantum Computing Terms

- **Qubit:**
  The basic unit of quantum information, analogous to a classical bit, but capable of being in a superposition of states.

- **Superposition:**
  A fundamental principle in quantum mechanics where a qubit can exist in multiple states simultaneously until measured.

- **Entanglement:**
  A quantum phenomenon where the states of two or more qubits become linked, such that the state of one qubit cannot be described independently of the state of the others.

- **Quantum Gate:**
  A basic operation that changes the state of a qubit. Examples include the Hadamard gate, Pauli-X, -Y, -Z gates, and controlled gates like CNOT.

- **Quantum Circuit:**
  A sequence of quantum gates applied to a set of qubits, representing a quantum algorithm.

- **Bloch Sphere:**
  A graphical representation of the state of a single qubit, showing the probabilities of measurement outcomes on a 3D sphere.

- **Unitary Operator:**
  An operator that preserves the norm of quantum states, representing reversible quantum operations.

- **Density Matrix:**
  A matrix that describes the statistical state of a quantum system, useful for representing mixed states.

- **Decoherence:**
  The process by which a quantum system loses its quantum behavior, often due to interactions with the environment.

.NET MAUI Terms

- **.NET MAUI:**
  .NET Multi-platform App UI, a framework for building cross-platform applications that run on Windows, macOS, iOS, and Android using a single codebase.

- **XAML:**
  eXtensible Application Markup Language used in .NET MAUI to declaratively define user interfaces.

- **MVVM:**
  Model-View-ViewModel, a design pattern that separates the user interface (View) from the business logic (Model) via an intermediary (ViewModel).

- **GraphicsView:**
  A control in .NET MAUI that enables custom drawing and rendering of

complex graphics, ideal for visualizing quantum states and circuits.

- **Data Binding:**
  The process of connecting UI elements in XAML to data sources in the ViewModel, enabling automatic updates and synchronization.

- **Layouts:**
  Containers in .NET MAUI (such as Grid, StackLayout, FlexLayout) used to organize UI elements across different screen sizes and orientations.

- **Shell:**
  A high-level container in .NET MAUI that simplifies navigation and organization of multi-page applications.

- **Custom Controls:**
  Developer-defined UI elements that encapsulate specific functionalities or visualizations, such as a custom Bloch sphere renderer.

- **Emulators and Simulators:**
  Tools that replicate the behavior of target platforms (Android, iOS, etc.) for testing and debugging purposes.

Additional Terms

- **API (Application Programming Interface):**
  A set of protocols and tools for building software applications. Quantum APIs allow access to quantum hardware and simulators.

- **Cloud-Based Quantum Services:**
  Services provided over the cloud (e.g., IBM Quantum, Azure Quantum) that allow users to run quantum computations remotely.

- **Concatenated Codes:**
  A technique in quantum error correction where a quantum code is applied

recursively to reduce error rates.

This glossary provides clear definitions to help you quickly reference and understand the key concepts and technical terms encountered in both quantum computing and .NET MAUI development. It serves as an invaluable tool for readers from diverse backgrounds—whether you are a physicist, a software developer, or a quantum computing enthusiast.

The appendices in this book are designed to be your go-to reference materials throughout your quantum computing and .NET MAUI development journey. Appendix A equips you with the mathematical language of quantum mechanics, Appendix B consolidates practical development resources and sample code, and Appendix C demystifies the technical vocabulary that spans these cutting-edge fields.

Together, these appendices not only reinforce the core content of the book but also empower you with the tools, knowledge, and references needed to explore and innovate at the intersection of quantum computing and cross-platform application development.